Elizabeth The Queen

THE STORY OF BRITAIN'S
NEW SOVEREIGN

Elizabeth The Queen

THE STORY OF BRITAIN'S
NEW SOVEREIGN

by MARION CRAWFORD

Author of *The Little Princesses*
Mother and Queen

GREENWOOD PRESS, PUBLISHERS
WESTPORT, CONNECTICUT

Part One

On the evening of November 14, 1948—a Sunday—my husband and I were sitting by the fireside of our home in Nottingham Cottage, Kensington Palace, listening to the nine-o'clock news. Listening, like millions of other people, for an announcement of world importance. It did not come, and then the rest of the news seemed not to matter.

George switched over to a musical program and I picked up the thriller I had been reading.

"The silence of the room," I read, *"was shattered by the shrill cry of the telephone bell."* And then my own telephone rang.

Before I picked up the receiver I had an idea what the news would be.

"Turn down the music, darling," I said to George.

He is a musician and really listens to music instead of merely letting it flow gently past him. He likes it to fill the room.

But this time he turned the radio right off and watched me at the telephone; I recognized Mr. Baker's voice. Mr. Baker is the Buckingham Palace telephone operator, chosen for, among other excellent qualities, his clear, cultured voice.

"Madam, Sir Dermot Kavanagh would like to speak to you," he said.

Sir Dermot is Crown Equerry, in charge of all the Royal horses and motorcars. I waited for his familiar, friendly voice.

Then, instead of his usually gentle tones, I heard him burst out exuberantly, "Crawfie, I wanted you to be the first outside the Palace to know. It's a boy!"

"I'm so glad!" I said.

I should have been glad just the same if the baby had been a girl. I was happy for Princess Elizabeth, for the baby, for everyone.

What is the first thing we should do when we hear that a baby is born? I did it almost instinctively—I said a little prayer for him and his mother. And I heard George say, "Thank God!" That was a prayer, too, with a wealth of meaning in it.

It was perhaps twenty minutes past nine when I hung up the receiver. Soon the bulletin would be ringing round the world. But for the moment George and I shared the precious privilege of being among the first to know that Princess Elizabeth had just given birth to a baby boy who, one day, would reign over us.

"You're relieved?" George asked, always quick to sense my mood.

"Don't be absurd," I said. "I always knew that Princess Elizabeth would do everything perfectly. I have never known her to fail at anything important."

So I begin my story from the point where I left off in my book *The Little Princesses.*

There I simply said: "I had a telephone message from Buckingham Palace informing me that Her Royal Highness had had a son."

Now I will tell the story more fully for the first time in setting out to write about Queen Elizabeth. And what can more reveal the woman than—motherhood?

In the corner of my drawing room, overlooking the quiet gray street in which I now live, there stands a small square mahogany box, considerably battered by time.

Often during the day my eye turns toward it, for there, below its lid, lie a hundred memories of the many years I spent with the Royal Family.

There, neatly tied in separate bundles, are the letters Queen Elizabeth and Princess Margaret have written to me over the years. There is that sprig of white heather Princess Elizabeth gave me on her sixth birthday when I had not been with her long and was somewhat overawed by the presence of all her Royal relatives. And there are those Christmas cards the Princesses painted themselves with such industry, and sent out to their friends and family with such excitement. There are a myriad memories of my seventeen years as Governess to the two Princesses.

I had the box made, I remember, after the Duchess of York, as the Queen Mother Elizabeth was then, had asked me to take a trial month with them. It was fashioned from the paneling in the wardroom of the German battleship *Prinz Regent Luitpold,* which had been scuttled by her crew in Scapa Flow after World War I, later raised and towed to Rosyth, near my home then in Dunfermline, to be broken up.

The box was constructed like a pirate's chest in miniature, bound with brass at the edges, with my initial M set in lighter wood in the center of the lid. It cost me three pounds. You would not get such work today for twenty pounds.

It would do, I thought, to carry my papers and a few books for the teaching post to which I felt sure I would return before long.

From that day to this it has never left my side. It was with me that morning, so many years ago, when I set off from the busy Scottish town of Dunfermline to that strange world of courtiers and courtesy which was to be mine for so long and from which I was to learn so much.

It moved with me from 145 Piccadilly on that fateful day when the two little Princesses and I followed in the wake of the Crystal Coach which was taking the King and Queen to their new home in Buckingham Palace.

There my box stood on the window sill of my room, in plain view, outlined against the net curtain, of passers-by on Constitution Hill. Often, as we drove by, Princess Elizabeth would look up and say, "Look, Crawfie. Your treasure chest!"

I cannot think of any more apt description for what it now contains.

And finally the box moved with me from my little Grace and Favour house in Kensington Palace, granted to me for life by His Majesty King George VI when I married and retired from the Royal Service, to this calm house where I now live and find some of the tranquillity denied me in the turmoil of Royal life in London.

Now the box rests at what I hope is the end of its journey. And here, I like to think, I shall be able to turn to it in future years and show that, in however small a way, I had a hand in the making of England's Queen.

So to return to that important telephone call to me from Buckingham Palace.

Just as I was one of the first to hear the actual news of the birth so I was among the first to know months before that a Royal baby was on the way.

One afternoon I was sitting down to tea in my rooms when there came a gentle knock at the door and Princess Elizabeth put her head in.

In my many years at the Palace I had become an experienced mood-gauger. Usually a certain un-Royal thump-thump of feet down the passage would warn me that the Princess had some good news to pass on. For example, my door would burst open and a very flushed and excited Princess would sweep in. "Oh, Crawfie," she would say. "Guess what? Papa's horse won again today."

But this day, despite her quietness, I knew that she had bigger news than horse racing. While I waited for it I invited her to have some tea.

"No, thank you, Crawfie," she said in the odd little voice that meant she was nervous or excited.

She crossed the room quietly and gazed out of the window. There was something about her stillness which spoke more than words. I looked thoughtfully at her back.

"I've just come to tell you something, Crawfie," she said after a pause.

I waited.

She chose her words carefully, still not looking at me. "I'm having the old pram brought out."

I went to her side quickly and put my arms round her. "I'm so happy for you, darling," I said. Then we kissed and wept a little. It seemed hard for me to believe that she was grown up enough to have a baby.

The birth of a Royal baby, especially when he is in direct line to the Throne, is an affair of State; but, of course, it is also very much a private affair. When the child is "expected," the waiting world must be told.

From that moment, months before the birth, the baby

is news, and he will be news all his life. The fierce light of publicity will be a burden hard to bear, as no one knows better than his mother, who must share her own joy with all the world.

For Princess Elizabeth there was only a little time—a few precious weeks—when she could nurse and enjoy her secret. We who were close to her knew, of course, before the first speculative hints appeared in the newspapers.

There was a new shine in her eyes, a radiance from within, which all of us in the Household were conscious of.

Soon others were to notice it. Indeed the radiance became so unmistakable that the newspapers took it almost as an unofficial announcement.

I can reveal now that there was some annoyance among members of the Household over these premature revelations. Some journalists abroad even went so far as to forecast, by "scientific" means, whether the child would be a boy or a girl. Some of these learned prognosticators pointed one way, and some the other, but one thing was certain: Princess Elizabeth was going to have a baby.

"Why can't they let her have her baby in peace?" growled members of the Household. As if that could be possible in a world filled with curiosity!

But it was not idle curiosity. The eagerness of everyone to know everything about Princess Elizabeth, to wish her well, to pray for her health and happiness, was a sign of their high regard for her. It must have been some recompense for the invasion of her privacy to realize that millions were praying for her.

The pram Princess Elizabeth had mentioned was a stately affair which should really have been called a perambulator, if not a carriage.

It was the one in which both she and Princess Margaret had been wheeled when children, and for which they hold a deep affection.

After speaking to me about it, someone was sent down to Windsor—that storehouse of Royal relics, from priceless dresses and jewels to baby shoes and christening robes—to dig it out. It was overhauled from top to bottom and was solemnly brought up to the Palace.

The first time that we tested it, in Princess Elizabeth's rooms, was an hilarious occasion. I was sent for, and as I came near I heard shrieks of laughter. Then I opened the door and saw Bobo, the Princess's personal maid, marching behind the empty pram with a look of pride.

The very upright, old-fashioned vehicle was paraded up and down before us. Bobo's pride was unmistakable but very understandable. It was like old times to her to be wheeling the pram in which she had taken Princess Elizabeth and then Princess Margaret for their airings from 145 Piccadilly.

While we were enjoying the spectacle Princess Margaret came in. When she saw what was happening she said delightedly, "Oh, the pram!"

She rushed forward, took it from Bobo and began wheeling it about herself, smiling happily.

Such pictures as those, coming into my mind today, seem to take away nothing of the Royal grandeur that surrounds Princess Elizabeth in her public life, but rather throw it into sharper relief.

All of us in the Palace were naturally concerned for the Princess as the time for the birth of her baby approached. But none of us had any fear that she would not come through her ordeal safely and happily. She is the sort of person who goes competently about any business that engages her, and she faced motherhood calmly.

One of the first things she did was to call in Sir William Gilliatt, her doctor, to explain everything to her. He told her what she ought to do, and she carefully followed the routine he set.

There were no extravagant or faddish preparations. She got up at her usual time and took her usual meals supplemented by plenty of green food and orange juice. She took no alcoholic drink of any sort.

That abstinence was easy for her, because she had never used liquor herself. At a cocktail party I have seen her nursing one drink through a long session, and leave it three parts untouched at the end. Smoking did not come into the matter, as she has never smoked. Prince Philip is equally abstemious.

All evening engagements were cut out; the Princess arranged to be in bed by ten o'clock every night.

Princess Margaret's reaction to all this was amusing—and charming. Normally she is more high-spirited than thoughtful, although she has moments of great kindness and perception.

But suddenly she seemed to realize what motherhood meant to a woman, and became tender and protective toward her sister, bringing cushions for her back and seeing that she was comfortably seated long before such care became necessary. Such solicitude, from one normally so effervescent, was touching.

Princess Elizabeth, of course, went her own way. She would have nothing of the old superstitious attitude which made an illness of pregnancy.

"It should be a natural process," she would say. "After all, it is what we are made for."

How different this attitude was from that which prevailed in Queen Victoria's time! Then, a Princess would have disappeared entirely from public view, to spend much of her time in bed. But Princess Elizabeth had many public duties she continued to perform—most important of which was a tour of France with Prince Philip in May, 1948.

She refused to listen to any suggestion that the tour should be canceled. "They have made their arrangements," she said, "and we cannot let them down."

Paris gave them a tumultuous reception. Parisians in thousands lined the streets, hailed her as *"La Belle Princesse"* and declared that she was the best ambassadress Britain had ever sent to France. They were particularly delighted to hear her speak excellent French, fluently, clearly, with hardly a trace of English accent.

Princess Elizabeth was as happy as the crowds and much flattered by their ovation. Nevertheless, it was an exhausting round of appearances for her at such a time.

Pomp and ceremony in a Princess's own country are familiar ground to her; but abroad there is a certain strangeness. In Paris the people wanted to see the Royal couple everywhere, against every background of the city.

There was a series of majestic drives through the wide streets, whose crowds cheered in a most un-Republican way. The Princess's wardrobe of dresses sent a ripple of excitement through the fashion capital.

Even M. Dior, that leader among dress designers, could find no fault. "She is magnificent," he told one of the Royal party. "I never knew from pictures that she could be so lovely or wear her clothes with such distinction."

At home the fashion writers grew lyrical. At Nottingham Cottage I examined photographs with which the papers were full, and remembered what an effort it used to be even to persuade the Princess to change into a new hat.

Someone, I knew, must have been at work, for the Princess was always conservative about her dress, and content to wear whatever was laid out for her.

I did not have to look far for the author of this new

chic. Prince Philip was beside her in more ways than one on this tour, as I shall show.

Friends of mine who accompanied the Royal couple noticed a new protectiveness had come over the Prince. Wherever they went he was always close by his wife's side, ready to give her a hand up some steps, or guide her by the elbow through a crowded place. It was a courteous display of husbandly affection at a time when she must have found it most rewarding.

And finally, as the climax to the tour, came the occasion on which she was to lay a wreath on the tomb of the Unknown Soldier. This was prefaced by a drive through the city in an open car.

The tomb was surrounded by ranks of soldiers, who clashed to attention as the Princess stepped a few paces forward to lay her wreath.

As she leaned forward, the crowds saw her sway, as if she was going to fall. But Prince Philip was at hand. As he saw her falter, he took a quick pace forward and caught her elbow to steady her. The incident was over in a second or two, but it was one that none who saw it will ever forget.

"It was as if there was no one else there but the two of them," one of my friends told me later. "She needed him, and he was there."

And then Prince Philip helped her back to her place while the bands played the national anthems.

Those who stood near them could see how anxiously he watched in case she should sway again. But she did not. It must have needed great courage to stand to rigid attention, feeling as she did.

The strain, in fact, did tell. On the way back through streets lined with people cheering her with undiminished vigor, the emotion became too much for the Princess.

All through the journey the crowds could plainly see the tears streaming from her eyes. She made no attempt to hide them; they were a gracious acknowledgment of the tribute the Parisians paid her.

And also, perhaps, relief after the strain she had imposed upon herself.

I remember another occasion which illustrates the same determination in the Queen to see things through, however great the strain and however arduous the task.

Queen Elizabeth has always disliked the sea, which makes her odd man out in a circle of sailors.

Her father was a naval officer; so was his father before him; and so is her husband, the Duke of Edinburgh. She has crossed the sea often—to South Africa, to the Channel Islands, and back from Canada. And yet I know that she has never been able to overcome her aversion to it.

When she was eight years old King George, who was then Duke of York, fell ill. For his convalescence the whole family moved to the Duke of Devonshire's house, Compton Place, Eastbourne.

It is a large, rambling house which you come upon suddenly in the center of the town. But behind it lies a pleasant garden, and beyond that a wood which stretches up to a golf course.

We took great pleasure in that wood which the gardener had planted with hyacinths taken from the greenhouse, so that one would come upon a group of vivid colors all mixed up together, with the hyacinths, daffodils, and other flowers.

It was while at Eastbourne that Queen Elizabeth first came to know the sea. She had seen it before—when she went down to Bognor Regis to cheer her ailing "Grandpa England," as she called King George V.

But she had little memory of that. We used, at first, to go to the private beach chalet which went with the house. There we would make tea and fight off two huge dogs which always tried to make off with our rations.

Until too many people came to watch the Princesses play it was pleasant there. But despite the fun she had on the beach Queen Elizabeth never liked the sea. Something about the movement of the water seemed to spell danger to her.

If her father approached it too closely, she would scream to warn him. I think it rather puzzled the King, who so loved the sea himself, that his daughter should find it strange and alarming.

"It's the noise," she explained to me, "and the way it keeps rolling about and jumping at you."

Later, when we were making a cruise in that old-fashioned vessel, the Royal Yacht *Victoria and Albert*, which rolled and pitched in every direction, Princess Elizabeth was still landlubber enough to wish all the time that she was ashore.

With the Duke of Edinburgh, years later, she paid an official visit to the Channel Islands. Memories of the Nazi occupation were still vivid there and the coming of the Princess eagerly awaited.

On the morning she sailed in H.M.S. *Anson* I looked at the skies, and my heart grieved for her. Ashore, the weather was bad enough, but it was much worse in the Channel. I knew that the voyage in a rough sea would be a nightmare to her.

My fears proved true.

She was white with seasickness and almost prostrate when the ship dropped anchor off Sark.

Between the ship and the shore was a strip of angry sea, which had to be crossed in one of the ship's boats.

"Are you sure you're fit to go ashore?" asked her husband. She could not speak, but looked up at him and nodded.

On the quay the crowds saw the boat leave the ship's side and fight its way through the waves. They were deeply disappointed when they found that the Princess had been left behind—but not surprised.

In her place, General "Boy" Browning, the ex-Commando General who had been appointed Comptroller of the Princess's Household, stepped ashore.

The onlookers saw him talking for a few minutes with

officials. Then the boat pushed off and made for the ship again.

Aboard the *Anson,* the Princess's advisers doubted that she was fit to land. When she realized what they were saying she roused herself.

"Of course I am going ashore," she said. "I won't disappoint all those people."

A cheer rose from the islanders waiting on the quayside when they saw her descend the ladder, followed by Prince Philip, who held her arm to steady her.

As the little boat surged up on the crest of the swell to the quayside, the Princess made ready to jump ashore. But before she could do so the boat was down in the trough of the wave again, with the quayside looming high above.

After two attempts had failed, she tried again.

Philip stood beside her. As the boat rose he signaled to General Browning, and at exactly the right moment gave the Princess a little push, which sent her right into the General's waiting arms.

"Your Royal Highness ought to rest for a while," said the island's doctor who had been waiting with the crowds, knowing she might need his kindly aid.

She shook her head. "Give me two aspirins and a glass of water," she said. "I shall be all right."

A few moments later she climbed into the horse carriage which was to bear her round the island, for there are no motorcars on Sark.

The crowd of islanders cheered. The Princess smiled back at them.

They little knew the effort it cost her.

It was only four days after the momentous telephone message to me from Buckingham Palace, announcing the arrival of Princess Elizabeth's baby, that I saw Prince Charles, as he was to be named later.

It was in the afternoon, just as I was getting ready to leave the Palace. As I have explained, I was already living at Nottingham Cottage; my rooms at the Palace had been taken over by Prince Philip so that he could be near his wife at the time of the birth.

But I was still going daily to the Palace to sit with Princess Margaret and discuss whatever subjects came up. The strict schoolroom routine, such as we had known in the past, had been abandoned.

I knew that my real work as Royal Governess at the Palace was over.

But in the new, busy life which Princess Margaret was leading, her mother thought an hour or two of quiet, unrestrained chat on general subjects might soothe her.

On this afternoon I found that she had already gone off to some engagement. I was just putting on my hat and thinking about a small piece of Spode china I had seen that morning in an antique shop off Kensington High Street.

It would go well, I thought, on the low sill of my

sitting room. I was already planning its capture when Sister Rowe came into the room.

Sister Rowe is a kindly looking, capable woman who habitually wears the uniform of her profession—white cap, blue cotton dress, and starched apron. I was always particularly impressed by her cuffs, which were starched to the stiffness of steel and sat on her wrists like handcuffs. She had a very pleasant, low voice. I could imagine it soothing generations of babies.

"Oh, Miss Crawford, Princess Elizabeth would very much like you to see the baby now," she said. "She asked me particularly to find you."

Like all of us at the time, she called the Prince "The Baby." I had a feeling that to Sister Rowe he would always be just that.

Names, I suspect, do not matter much to her. It is His Majesty the Baby with whom she is concerned. To her, every baby is a king. But the thought that she was dealing here with a real and future king must have added zest to her task.

I quickly abandoned thoughts of my Spode and followed her along the corridor. The baby lay in the large, airy room which had been Prince Philip's dressing room. The blinds were drawn, but it was not too dark to see the baby clothes hung round the fireplace—just as they might be in any other nursery.

The cot stood to the right against the wall. It was an impressive affair, shaped like one of those you see in the illustrations to the stories of Hans Andersen. It was slung on a cream enameled metal frame under a sort of hood from which hung a double curtain of elaborately trimmed cream organdie. It was the same cot that Queen Elizabeth had lain in twenty-two years before.

The room was very still and smelled of soap. Sister Rowe led the way toward the cot, her apron rustling crisply as she moved. It was clear she thought the baby marvelous.

He lay on one cupped hand, sleeping quietly. The other small curled fist, no bigger than a buttercup it seemed, lay over the coverlet. To me he looked oddly like King George V.

"He's lovely," I said.

"We think so," said Sister Rowe. She stressed the "we" in an oddly moving way.

Could that little golden-haired girl I remembered in so many engaging scenes really have grown up to be the mother of this Royal child?

As I stared down into the cot, memories floated before me.

Soon Sister Rowe brought me back to the present. She whispered, a forefinger to her lips.

"We mustn't disturb him," she said.

Together we tiptoed to the door.

When I got home I sat down with George to write the Princess a note to tell her that I had seen the baby.

"He is a lovely child," I wrote. "You must be very proud of him."

With the note I enclosed a box of peppermint creams, always the Princess's favorite sweet.

The next day she sent a note thanking me for the letter. She still found it hard, she said, to believe that the adorable baby was really hers. She had always heard that all mothers felt the same way and was so happy and proud of her new baby son. She was glad, too, to be told from so many quarters that his arrival had given happiness to so many people besides Prince Philip and herself.

Her letter seemed to me to complete fully my years with her. In that time I had watched her grow from childhood to girlhood, become a radiant bride, and now, the fulfillment of every woman, a proud mother.

Princess Elizabeth, before the baby was born, had the same rations as other expectant mothers—seven pints of milk a week from her supplementary ration card, half as much again for her meat ration as the normal book provided, and a bottle of cod-liver oil supplied through the Food Office every six weeks.

Friends would send her orange juice, which was then becoming less scarce, and she was lucky to have a constant supply of eggs from the Home Farm at Windsor.

For the first few months she fed the baby herself. She was anxious to give him as good a foundation for health as possible, knowing this to be of great importance.

Wednesday, December 15, 1948, was a cold, crisp day. I woke with some excitement and lay in my ac-

customed way, letting my eyes rove over the room for
a little while.

Outside the birds were very active, their chirps forming a sort of descant to the deeper rumble of the traffic
passing along Kensington High Street.

It was the morning of Prince Charles's christening
day.

George and I had received a special invitation, per-
sonally passed to us by the Master of the Household.
This was a great honor. The occasion was to be so
personal that no printed invitations were issued. It was
to be "family" only.

The invitations told us to come for three o'clock.
Then came another message postponing it by half an
hour.

The Royal Family were to have a family lunch party
and they feared it might continue a little longer than
they had anticipated. They did not want to keep anyone waiting.

Normally I would enter the Palace by the Privy Purse
door, which lies at the right-hand corner of the building as you look at it from the Mall. But this was a special occasion, and we were driven right through one
of the center arches into the Inner Court.

A footman, clad in scarlet coat and white silk knee
breeches, came down the few steps from the Grand
Entrance and opened the car door.

He gave us a pleasant smile of greeting and then directed the chauffeur where to leave the car.

At garden parties or other functions there are so many cars that they have to drop their passengers and then wait outside along the Mall, from which they are summoned by loud-speaker. But there was no such crush this afternoon, and our car was allowed to wait in the Inner Court.

The Grand Hall with its crimson carpet and impressive statues is an imposing place.

That afternoon it was lined with footmen in the same splendid panoply as those at the door. I rather regretted that their powdered wigs had been abandoned before my time at the Palace.

Instead, the footmen now appear in their uniform with their hair caked with flour. I often used to wonder how this was done without also sprinkling their uniforms.

One pictures them putting their heads through a kind of stock which fits closely round their necks, while a comrade dabs them carefully with a powder puff. It must be a difficult operation, and messy to remove.

We marched along the Grand Hall and up the wide staircase, where we were met by General Sir Frederick Browning.

He smiled at us pleasantly. "The Queen wants everyone to go in and sit down," he said. "There is to be no fuss. Everything is to be as simple as possible."

Sir Frederick Browning showed us into the Gold and Silver Music Room. It was a place we had often used for dancing classes when the Princesses were small. It has a beautiful parquet floor upon which the troupe of little girls would pirouette with rocky enthusiasm.

. I remember that one day Sir Hill Child, then Master of the Household, came up to me after household lunch.

"I suppose you know, Miss Crawford," he began, "that the dancing lessons are ruining the floor in the Music Room? The parquets are springing up all over the place."

After that we had to find somewhere else to practice.

But now the room was richly laid out. It has high mirrored walls leading up to a domed ceiling. At the far end stood the font, decorated with white carnations and gardenias, sprinkled with a few green sprays of smilax.

About thirty chairs were set out in rows as if in a chapel. Sir Frederick Browning led us to them. "Sit anywhere you like," he said, "except in the front row. That is being kept for the Royal Family."

Then he took me by the arm. "You must be able to see properly, Crawfie," he said in his kind way, and showed us to an aisle seat in the second row.

We were among the early comers. I thought that we might be a little in the way. So a moment or two later we moved back into the third row.

Gradually the seats began to fill. Several of the Queen's relatives were there and a number of Court Officials. The Lord Chamberlain, Lord Clarendon, came and sat down right in front of us, while I saw Bobo and Ruby MacDonald—sister of Bobo and Princess Margaret's personal maid—very smartly dressed, take their seats together a little behind us.

Presently in came a file of choirboys, very pretty in their red and white cassocks and cottas, led by the Organist to the Chapel Royal.

He marched straight to the beautiful old French grand piano which stood at the left of the font, halfway between the font and the front row, and began to play softly.

It was, I remember, the piano on which Princess Margaret had so often played Brahms's Cradle Song. I wondered if she would remember that now.

When the Archbishop of Canterbury came in, we all stood up. We seemed to remain like that for a very long time. Then he smiled and said, "I think you had better all sit down."

Presently the Royal Family entered, led by the King and Queen. We all stood up again and watched them file to their seats in front of us, closely followed by Sister Rowe carrying the baby. It was so nice to hear, as she passed, that same comforting rustle from her apron.

I was, I recall, a little concerned about Princess Elizabeth. She did not look very well. She was wearing a cherry-colored coat and hat, but she seemed to me to be a little tired.

I saw that she settled into her seat rather gratefully. I hoped she had not overstrained herself. She never will spare herself if there is work to be done.

The service lasted half an hour. The King and Queen,

Princess Elizabeth, Prince Philip, and the Duchess of Kent sat on the left-hand side of the front row; the Earl and Countess of Athlone, Princess Margaret and Queen Mary on the other.

The sponsors, among whom were Princess Margaret and the Queen's brother, the Hon. David Bowes-Lyon, were provided with printed guides to the questions the Archbishop would ask them.

I was concerned when the Archbishop took the baby in the crook of his arm. It seemed a very unsafe place, as if the slightest movement would dislodge the baby. But throughout the ceremony Prince Charles—as he became then—lay quiet as a mouse.

Even when the Archbishop poured three very ample shellfuls of water over the baby's head the Prince did not murmur.

Afterward there was a reception in one of the large drawing rooms next door. It was nice to see several of the old retainers, including the King's nannie, who had been specially invited.

The actual christening, which was most moving, had been a small, intimate affair. But there must have been two or three hundred people at the reception.

Sister Rowe carried the baby round for everyone to see. We stood by the fire, for the day was cold, talking to young Princess Alexandra, daughter of the Duchess of Kent. She is a very sprightly, charming child, with a personality which will certainly make its mark.

We also spoke with the Archbishop. I told him of my fear that he might drop the baby.

"You needn't have been worried," he said genially. "I'm an old hand at christenings. I once did nine in one afternoon, and not a casualty among them."

Part Two

"WHEN I get married, Crawfie, I shall make my husband as happy as Mummy has made Papa."

I thought of these words, spoken so earnestly to me by Princess Elizabeth in the nursery at 145 Piccadilly, years before when, soon after my own marriage, Princess Elizabeth and Prince Philip were among my very first visitors at Nottingham Cottage.

In preparing for a little party one evening, which was to fill my tiny cream-walled sitting room, I had been in a whirl of activity, running here and there to be sure that I had enough food, plenty of glasses, and a good stock of those little sausages on sticks which everyone seems to like.

All the people I had invited were my close friends; I was most anxious for everything to go smoothly. Every woman will understand that.

Then the bell rang. I went to the door and to my astonishment found my first visitors were the young Royal couple, newly married!

Much later, I remember looking up for a moment from a bottle I was trying to open. Mechanical things are not in my line, and I hoped to catch the eye of my husband George, who is the sort of man for whom knots untie themselves without help and can openers become sharp.

Instead of George, I caught sight of Prince Philip, standing facing the room, his head just below a picture of myself, done in charcoal by David Gunn—"Pop" Gunn we used to call him.

It had been done before I joined the Royal Family, showing the Eton crop hair style that I was still wearing when I first set eyes on the little girl who was to become Duchess of Edinburgh, Heiress to the Throne.

I saw Prince Philip look, for a long moment, at Princess Elizabeth with an expression of tender affection which touched me deeply. There was, perhaps, fifteen feet between them, but to them there was clearly no division at all. To this day I never see this portrait of myself without recalling this incident.

I remembered the early impression Prince Philip had made on me, and my surprise when I discovered how wrong I had been.

At first I thought him a noisy, overexcited young fellow, eager to make himself seen and heard. It was before the war, and he was very young. I see now that he was only eager to please.

When he first began to appear on the scene again during the war—always in naval uniform—something of that first impression still lingered.

But soon, as he was seen more and more at the Palace, I found that he had grown up delightfully, with charming manners and a wide interest in important matters not always closely studied by a young naval officer.

But toward the end of the war and later, when rumors of the forthcoming engagement were rife and Prince Philip was seen more often at the Palace, he was discussed by members of the Household.

This, after all, was natural. People who have spent their lives in the services of the King and Court may be expected to be passionately interested in the future husband of the King's daughter.

But they knew little more of what was really happening than the people in the street had gathered from gossip based on newspaper hints.

I remember one night at dinner a crusty old gentleman asked the company at table, "Who is this young fellow? What does anybody know about him?"

No one could say much about him from hard knowledge, but there was a good deal of the same sort of gossip that was bandied about wherever people met.

Was it true that he was rather high-spirited? Inclined to resent discipline?

"That certainly isn't so," I said.

Later I was glad to have my opinion confirmed by a senior naval officer who dined one night with the Household.

He told us, when the conversation turned that way, that the Navy had a high regard for "young Philip."

"He is a natural seaman," was the way he put it. "He does his job quickly and efficiently. And he is popular, both in the wardroom and below decks. I'd say he'll end up an admiral, like his uncle."

He meant Lord Louis Mountbatten, of course, one of the finest officers the Navy has ever had.

Lord Louis brought Prince Philip up when his parents decided that they wished him to have the benefit of a British schooling. It must have been from him that Prince Philip caught his love of the sea and ships.

That Prince Philip was a capable naval officer was certainly in his favor when he was discussed by the Household. One question that was never raised in that company was, "Is it a love match?" For it obviously was.

It may be hard for people who did not watch, as we did, the growth of love between the two young people, to realize what a natural, unsponsored affection it was.

True, Prince Philip, as a Prince of Royal blood, was one of the very small set of eligible young men who could ask the Princess's hand in marriage.

But I do not believe that if the King had a free

choice of sons-in-law he would have settled on Prince Philip for that reason alone.

While the young people were serving an exacting apprenticeship for marriage, they were kept on tenterhooks. Would they, or would they not, be allowed to marry?

That was the question which not only they, but all their friends and most of the world, were asking.

There was never any question of their love for each other.

At that time Prince Philip was staying at Buckingham Palace. Most mornings he took breakfast with the Household. He would come in hurriedly, eat his food, and hurry out, having exchanged not more than half-a-dozen words with anybody. Of course he was a man on trial for a most exalted post, and he had much on his mind.

Also he was in love.

But absorbed as he must have been with his private concerns, the natural charm of his manner won over those who at first had wondered whether he was really a suitable match for Princess Elizabeth.

There was something very engaging about his lack of formality. He liked to go to the back of the Palace, where the stables and garages are, and clean and tune up his little sport car.

The chauffeurs loved him for it, but they were always chary when he wanted to borrow one of the Royal cars and give it a "tryout on the road."

Royal cars are not used to sporting treatment. They like to roll along safely and sedately; but no one knows what would happen if they were ever given their heads.

Sometimes Princess Elizabeth would join Prince Philip at the stables. Although she had little interest in mechanical contrivances, she loved to see him lift the bonnet of his car and, with oily hands, adjust the engine.

Indeed, it has always been a great pleasure to me to see Queen Elizabeth and Prince Philip together. She always seemed brighter when he was about; their happiness seemed to light up the whole Palace. So, when the engagement was announced and the wedding fixed, everyone was delighted.

It was all settled now. No longer was there need to deny gossip. Before the engagement, when nothing was decided, the Princess had had many uncomfortable moments in public when she had overheard remarks about a possible "love match."

The coming wedding was an event of historic and world-wide importance. Preparations for the occasion brought great activity to Buckingham Palace. Although my own work was finished, I considered it a privilege to be allowed to go on helping as much as I could.

Princess Elizabeth's engagement period was an exhausting time for her. There were so many things to attend to that she simply had to break off sometimes. Occasionally she would come along the corridor to my room for a chat.

Then, as in the old days, she would put her feet up while we talked, or I read to her. Or sometimes I would go along to her room.

The Palace is an exciting place to live in, with people always in and out of your room on one errand or another; and it was more so at that time than ever.

Once, I remember, I had been disturbed so often that I felt I could stand no more interruptions. There was a very charming footman who brought my tea every day.

He was a delightful man and always very polite, but this time I felt that I could not face even him. As I heard him coming, I ran into the bathroom and locked myself in. I heard him wandering about rather uncertainly for a few minutes; then he went out. When I unlocked the door, I found that he had left the tray for me.

The Princesses, who had been brought up to this life, hardly noticed such interruptions. But if Princess Elizabeth and I wanted to talk quietly for a while, we had to take the dogs for a walk in the garden. Often we talked of our future homes. There was this new and added bond between us.

For Queen Elizabeth was planning her first home at the time when I was planning mine. I had been married just one month when I sat with my husband in Westminster Abbey and saw the little girl I had

· 37

watched growing to regal womanhood married to the man of her choice.

Through all the pageantry and music I thought of the truest meaning of a wedding—the making of a home.

I remembered the Princess saying to me, as she looked up from a heap of patterns she was studying, "Do you think that the blue or the beige would go better in this room?"

She was speaking then of Sunninghill Park, which not long after was to be burned to the ground. But we often spoke of my own little home, Nottingham Cottage, which was being got ready at the same time.

Opposite the front door of that same cottage was the very door from which Prince Philip stepped out on his wedding morning.

And from my window above I would often see also a figure dressed in gray, with a sort of nun's veil round her head. This was Princess Andrew of Greece, Lord Mountbatten's sister, and the mother of Prince Philip.

Sometimes I would pass her on the walks leading from Kensington Palace as she went out to do her shopping, and I would wish her a good morning. Most often she would smile an answer, but sometimes, probably wrapped in thought, she would not seem to realize anything of her surroundings.

The high cost of everything appalled Princess Elizabeth when she was planning her home. She and

Princess Margaret had been brought up to be careful with money. With goods too.

In furnishing her home, Princess Elizabeth was able to draw on stocks of material that her mother, a careful buyer, had accumulated. Much of it had been bought before the war at the British Industries Fairs and other exhibitions.

Nothing that comes to the Royal Family, by purchase or gift, is ever wasted. Everything is labeled and put away, safe from moths and other dangers, and catalogues are kept of all the Royal possessions, so that when anything is needed it may be available at once.

Princess Elizabeth would say to me, "Mummy says she has something that might do for this corner. That will save a little expense anyway."

The Queen was very kind to me in this way too. She allowed me to choose several pieces to take to my own first home.

"Have anything you like, Crawfie," she was good enough to say; and I spent many delightful hours assessing the merits of various pieces of furniture in relation to my tiny rooms of the cottage.

In the end I chose a tall combined china cupboard and desk and a mahogany table, among several other things, and these became the most admired pieces in my dining room.

All through my Palace years, when I was moving to and from London, Windsor, and occasionally Balmoral, I was constantly haunted by a desire to have a place of my own; to be able to come down to a kitchen where *my* cups were laid out, to find *my* cutlery stacked neatly in a drawer, to eat at my own table.

For years I collected things for a home that did not yet exist. I would search the antique shops in Church Street, Kensington, for pieces of china and other articles that appealed to me. To get something for less than I thought it was worth was a great thrill.

It gave me a sense of achievement, a feeling that so many pounds or shillings had been saved—forgetting that there had been no real need to spend money at all.

But in this way I surrounded myself with belongings which gave me, even in the gloomy, impersonal recesses of Buckingham Palace, a feeling of having an individual private life.

But I know that a cupboard or two full of my own china would never take the place of a real home. So you can imagine with what excitement I looked forward to marriage and a home of my own, at the same time when Queen Elizabeth was planning hers.

When I did eventually move into Nottingham Cottage I often changed the layout of the furniture in the rooms. In the middle of something else I would suddenly get up and say, "I think that little easy chair would look better on the right of the fireplace"—and immediately go over and place it there. George, my husband, found this hard to understand, but smiled indulgently.

As every woman knows, it is usually the wife who

spreads oil on the troubled waters of a marriage. She likes to hear her husband praised, hates to feel a tension growing in her house when he is cross or short with visitors, as may well happen if he is not well. Men are very vocal about their aches and pains.

How much greater is the strain on a Royal wife! I have a deep admiration for Prince Philip as a grown man. He has qualities I greatly admire, but many of them are not fashioned for Court use. He is frank and outspoken, keen to be on with the next thing, and impatient of flattery. He hates unnecessary fuss and all publicity.

The fanfare which heralds his every move now must be torture to him. But it was the small price he gladly paid for marrying the woman he loved—to step out of the cheerful, semi-obscurity of the Navy into the brightest spotlight the world has ever known.

But one sometimes forgets. It is then that the wife has to step forward and smooth the path. Like her mother, Queen Elizabeth has this quality of sympathetic tact, highly developed.

"Come on, darling," her eyes seem to say. "Stick it just a little while longer."

Few who have not seen the effect it may have can appreciate the strain of always living in the public eye. When you or I marry we make our arrangements in private, marry among our friends and relatives, and honeymoon quietly in the place of our choice. But for Royalty things are never so simple.

Even while on their honeymoon Princess Elizabeth and Prince Philip were pestered by photographers and curious tourists who made special journeys to try to catch a glimpse of them.

It was not until they at last got up to Birkhall, a house belonging to the King near Balmoral, that they were able to be really alone.

The native courtesy of the Scots countryfolk showed itself in their tact. They left the Royal couple entirely to themselves.

It was winter, and snow was on the ground. Princess Elizabeth wrote me a charming letter. The countryside was lovely, she said, far more beautiful than it had been when we were up there at about the same time of year at the beginning of the war. They had a new puppy, Rummy, with them, who was enjoying himself romping about in the snow.

It must have been a very happy time for them, left completely alone together for the first time in their lives.

But that particular kind of "being alone" happiness could not last long; soon they were back in the center of things, doing their great work in the world.

It has become much easier for me to see the Princess as a person since I left the Palace and began my married life in the first home of my own I have ever had.

What matters most to all of us now is the character of

the woman who, by the grace of God, now guides the destiny of ours and other lands.

How often we see her smiling! Her smile is as much part of her as her lovely complexion and the features that startlingly recall to most people the pictures of the great Queen Victoria when she was young.

I see other resemblances as well. She is very like her aunt, Lady Rose Granville, who had a home at Dunfermline, not far from my mother's house.

Later, Lady Rose and her husband moved to London and took a pleasant, narrow house at 100 Park Street, where I used to go when I felt the need of peace and quiet.

Lady Rose was very understanding. She knew how greatly I missed my Scottish hills, and how I liked sometimes to be alone.

She gave me a latchkey to the house. "Use the place whenever you wish," she said in her charming, soft voice, so like the Queen's. "It may not bring you the heather, but at least you will be quiet here."

Lady Rose is one of the most beautiful women I have ever seen. Even in middle age her skin is perfect. The artist Laszlo has captured it in a portrait which hung over the drawing room fireplace of the London house.

I knew that picture long ago when Queen Elizabeth was a child. Even then how like she was to her aunt! And as the child grew up she resembled more and more the lovely woman of the picture, with gracious, curving neck and shining, candle-clear complexion—an almost ethereal skin, through which the warmth of health seems to shine.

And still there is that inescapable resemblance to Queen Victoria, who was so beautiful as a young woman. I remember an old friend of the Royal Family saying to me, as we watched the crowds swirling round the Princess at one of the first garden parties at Buckingham Palace after the war:

"When I was a child I saw Queen Victoria pass in a coach. Although she was very old then, she had in her eyes a calm confidence and determination which I have often seen mirrored in the eyes of Princess Elizabeth."

The remark surprised me a little at the time it was spoken. I had too many happy memories of Princess Elizabeth flushed with laughter, romping in the school-room or garden, to see her as a Queen.

But now that I have watched her come into womanhood and take on the Royal dignity that belongs to her, I am convinced that the man at the garden party was right.

There are other things I have remembered, too, as I've watched Princess Elizabeth and her husband Prince Philip together.

I have thought of the responsibilities the Princess must bear at the same time as her duties as a wife and mother.

It was just as much of a trial for her to have her husband overseas making his tour of duty in Malta as it would have been for any other naval officer's wife.

At the same time she had to carry an increasing load of responsibility temporarily lifted from her father's shoulders.

When she at last found time to fly out to her husband, some people were openly critical. No one would have questioned the right of another naval wife to do the same thing, providing she left her children in good hands.

Was Princess Elizabeth to be less a wife because she was Heiress to the Throne?

Surely her stature is the greater because she is indeed a good wife and mother.

And what babies in the world have been left in better hands than those which care for Prince Charles and his sister Princess Anne? Later I shall show with what kindness they are tended, by two capable nurses, under the watchful, loving eye of their grandmother.

And Prince Philip, who is a sailor before he is a courtier, is above all a good father, anxious for his children's welfare.

He has lived his life among men who judge one another by their real worth. When he took command of the frigate *Magpie* in the Mediterranean, he was the youngest Lieutenant-Commander in the flotilla.

A naval friend of mine told me that, though he was always popular in the Navy, there were some who thought his appointment sprang from privilege. They expected him to be "nursed" by an experienced first lieutenant.

But they were wrong, as Prince Philip quickly showed them.

When he left his ship to come home, his crew felt that they had lost not only a brilliant Captain, but also a close friend.

For a naturally proud and regal person, Prince Philip has a strange simplicity of approach. I have never seen him other than courteous and correct to everyone. And if he ever meets a shipmate of whatever rank, who has served with him, he is always quick to speak to him, wherever the two of them are.

In this way he introduced to the King and Queen an old friend he saw in the crowd surrounding the Royal Family at a garden party. And similarly, at a reception for the Royal couple in Nottingham, he met the man who had been his personal servant in H.M.S. *Wallace* during the war. They chatted together for a few minutes. Then the man said, "I would like to introduce my wife, sir."

Prince Philip looked at the woman. "I hope you are taking as good care of him as he used to of me," he said, and went on: "Now you must meet my wife."

Princess Elizabeth was at the other side of the room. Prince Philip went over to fetch her. "I should like you to meet some friends of mine, darling," he told her.

Then he introduced the waiting couple to her. "This is my wife," he said.

What were Princess Elizabeth's own thoughts about love?

Plenty of romances have been written about the loves of Princesses, but the settings are foreign and strange, and the Princesses are nothing at all like real Princesses.

The story of the factory girl who is loved by a Lord and becomes a Marchioness can hardly thrill a girl to whom Marchionesses must curtsy.

The love of a real Princess is important not only to herself and to the man she chooses, but also to millions of other people. It is an affair of State.

And yet, as we have seen, it can be truly a love affair. It certainly is so with Queen Elizabeth and Prince Philip.

In the days when Princess Elizabeth first questioned me about love and marriage, there was no thought in anyone's mind that she would ever be married to the young Prince of Greece and Denmark, who could speak neither Greek nor Danish, but was known to be a first-class cricketer and a keen yachtsman.

That the Heiress to the Throne would stay unmarried was unthinkable. The first Queen Elizabeth went unwed throughout her life; but times had changed since then.

So our Princess Elizabeth in due course of events would marry—but whom? The field could not be wide. Only a very few can be considered when the question of choosing a husband for a future Queen arises.

There was a great deal of guesswork and speculation, but from my own observation I must say now that no serious effort was made to choose a husband for Princess Elizabeth.

The choice was her own.

Naturally, as any girl growing into womanhood does, Queen Elizabeth often spoke to me of love and marriage. Far from avoiding the subject, I welcomed it.

It seemed to me that at this time, long before her engagement, such a discussion would be of help to her only as it was then possible to talk of marriage as woman to woman detachedly and without the introduction of any personalities.

Whenever she asked me questions, I tried to answer as truthfully and clearly as possible. In her own circle, she had, of course, seen only happy marriages, and she was anxious that her own marriage, when the time came, should follow this pattern.

"What, Crawfie," she would ask, "makes a person fall in love?"

Then I would try to explain to her the deep common interests that cannot only first draw a man and a woman together immediately, but hold them together for life.

"When you marry," I once told her, "you must not expect the honeymoon to last forever. Sooner or later you will meet the stresses and strains of everyday life. You must not expect your husband to be constantly at your side or always to receive from him the extravagant affection of the first few months.

"A man has his own men friends, hobbies, and interests in which you can not and will not want to share. A man's life is built on the foundation of a happy marriage. A good wife realizes that and will help him in every way she can."

The Princess listened attentively to these words. But she had read and heard there were homes without that atmosphere of love and affection which had surrounded her all her life.

One morning I found her depressed. The newspapers were full of the divorce of an acquaintance of hers, whose children she was very fond of.

"Why do people do it, Crawfie?" she asked me. "How can they break up a home when there are children to consider?"

It was difficult for her, who had never seen anything but the perfection of her parents' home life, to realize that some personalities are incompatible, some homes unhappy.

But since there were such people, she asked, why did they get married in the first place?

She was deeply distressed by this. I tried to explain to her that many marriages had been contracted in wartime, on impulse alone, without reasonable reflection or true love.

I tried to explain that the shortage of houses made marriage difficult for some people. It is hard for a Princess brought up in a Palace with endless rooms to appreciate that. But she tried to.

We must remember now that a Royal Princess has nothing like the same freedom to fall in love and marry that most other girls have. Most of the romances she reads are about a world that she does not and can never know, about people of different backgrounds who meet and part, quarrel and make it up again, as a Princess, trained to self-control, cannot do.

Queen Elizabeth was never a great reader of love stories. Almost instinctively her taste led her to well-written works, true to life.

But where could she find stories true to her own sort of life?

When I hear of Hollywood stars who complain that successful marriage is impossible for people like themselves, "Living in a goldfish bowl" and never having a minute to themselves, I stop and think of the much greater trials Princess Elizabeth and Prince Philip have had to face in their marriage.

Part Three

FRIENDS often ask me how things are arranged at Buckingham Palace. Who does what, for instance, and how? Is there someone for every job that has to be done?

Indeed there is, as I shall show.

One day Princess Elizabeth came to me very worried because she had been kept awake most of the night by the scraping and scratching of a mouse.

"I'll send for the Vermin Man," I said.

"Oh, Crawfie, do you have to? Couldn't we just catch it ourselves," she said, "and then let it loose in the garden? I'm sure it doesn't mean any harm."

I am not so scared of mice as some women. I can remember the pleasure I used to get from watching their activities in the fields around my grandmother's house at Gatehead. But I did not welcome the prospect of spending half the night on my knees coaxing a mouse into a bag and then smuggling it out into the garden.

"I think we'd better get expert advice," I said. "He knows how to do it better than we do."

The Lord Chamberlain's Office publishes a little book stamped with the Crown entitled, "Offices and Addresses of Their Majesties' Households and Officers of State and other Royal Households."

It is known in the Palace as the Green Book, and contains, as it says, the names and addresses of all who work in or are connected with the Royal houses.

It is a very useful volume, because one can turn in a second to the appropriate person to solve any problem.

There in the front is a list of the Cabinet, followed by a list of Ministers not in the Cabinet. Then comes a detailed list of the Royal Household, starting off in alphabetical order with the Aides de Camp, First and Principal Naval—through to Keepers of the King's Archives, Resident Factor at Balmoral, Clerk of the Closet, Equerries, Extra Equerries, Gentlemen Ushers, and so on for seventy-two pages.

If one is ill in the Palace, one only has to turn to "Physicians to the Household" and ring the doctor named to get the best possible attention.

But there are several people who attend the Household whose names do not figure in the Green Book.

The Vermin Man is one.

Like most old buildings with many cupboards and corridors, Buckingham Palace is on constant guard against mice. If you even thought you had heard one in your room, or if there were more concrete proof of their presence, all you had to do was summon the Vermin Man and he would undertake to rid your room of the pest.

So directly after breakfast I told the footman that we wanted to see the Vermin Man and would he please ask him to come to Princess Elizabeth's rooms after lunch?

At two-thirty exactly there came a knock on the door and the man appeared, carrying his tools in a large bag.

He inspected the floorboards and wainscot and said he saw definite evidence of a mouse being there. Then he brought out his traps and asked the Princess which she preferred.

One was the ordinary kind with a spring clip which is released when the mouse tries to get the piece of cheese it carries as bait.

The other was what he called the Treacle Trap. It was built on a piece of wood about a foot square covered with a sticky mess of glue-like substance surrounding a little platform on which was some food flavored with aniseed.

Apparently aniseed is as irresistible to mice as it is to dogs. "The mouse is lured by the smell," the man explained. "It tries to get to the aniseed, and is caught in the treacle."

"What happens after that?" asked Princess Elizabeth.

"It is trapped and dies through exhaustion in trying to get away," the man said.

I saw the Princess shudder and knew that the thought of the little creature fighting for its life would torture her.

But even though she felt the trap to be repulsive, she would not hurt the man's feelings.

"I'll have the other sort," she said, without comment.

It is hard for a sensitive person whose feelings are a barometer upon which other people's hard-luck stories play to keep their sympathetic approach.

Mothers would often write to Princess Elizabeth appealing to her to get their sons out of jail. "He has so little and you have so much. . . ."

And occasionally would come graver appeals for her to save a man sentenced to death. Always these letters would grieve her deeply.

She would try to understand why people committed crimes, and even when that was beyond her comprehension, still keep her sympathy for them.

"They don't know what they're doing," she would say. "No one could really kill another human being if he was in his right mind."

It distressed her that there was nothing she could do

to help these troubled mothers. All such letters were passed to the Home Office.

But no one who wrote to her, whatever the request, had the letter cast aside. Princess Elizabeth would always read the letters through most carefully, and I could tell from a certain thoughtful look that she was thinking about them very seriously.

Her friendship and sympathy are also positive. Shortly after we were married George fell ill and had to be taken to the hospital.

Knowing that he was musical and that we had no piano in Nottingham Cottage, Princess Elizabeth sent us her own miniature one, on which she had been taught as a child, so that George should have a pleasant surprise when he came home.

At the age of eighteen, three and a half years before her marriage, Princess Elizabeth came of age and achieved the dignity of a "Household" of her own, although of course she continued to live at the Palace.

For her it was the official end of girlhood and the beginning of her career as an important public figure. From then on, as one of the four Counsellors of State who would act for the King in his absence or other emergencies, she would take an increasing part in public affairs.

She was at the age when other girls could expect to enjoy new freedom of choice and action, to make new friends and to go about with them. For the Princess, her coming out meant also the assumption of new and heavy responsibilities.

It came to pass at a time—shortly before the Allied landing in Normandy—when many Royal activities had to be veiled in wartime secrecy.

For example, nothing could be revealed publicly of the visit the whole Royal Family made to H.M.S. *King George V* at Greenock, or of the Princess's return to Scotland a few weeks later, to launch at Clydebank the world's greatest battleship *Vanguard,* which in peacetime was to take the King and Queen and their daughters to South Africa.

That memorable tour was a foreshadowing of the visit of Princess Elizabeth and Prince Philip, as Duke and Duchess of Edinburgh, to Canada and the United States.

But already, at eighteen, she had been assigned her own armorial bearings consisting of the Royal Arms differenced by her own heraldic bearings, displayed on a lozenge instead of a shield—and her own Standard which flew wherever she went in Canada and the United States. It is the Standard which flew above Clarence House when she was at home.

From the end of the war Princess Elizabeth had her own Ladies-in-Waiting and her own Private Secretary. And immediately after her marriage General Sir Frederick Browning, K.B.E., C.B., D.S.O., was appointed Comptroller to her Household.

Sir Frederick had won great distinction by his war

service, and was best known for his gallantry and tenacity in command of the Airborne troops who fought so heroically at Arnhem. Married to the famous novelist, Daphne du Maurier, he was living quietly with her in Cornwall when he was summoned to Clarence House.

I had personal reasons to be pleased to hear of his appointment for I cherished an association with his charming sister, Miss Grace Browning, from the days when Princess Elizabeth and Princess Margaret, as children at Buckingham Palace, were enthusiastic members of the Palace Company of Girl Guides.

It was an unusual position for such a man of action to take. In the full health of his maturity, he was known as an intrepid soldier who might be expected to seek always a career of danger.

There was some talk among the Household about it. Some people wondered why such a man should accept a comparatively self-effacing post when others with far more opportunity for personal advantage must have been open to him.

But I welcomed the appearance of an experienced man whose interests lay outside Court routine. I thought he would bring Princess Elizabeth a breath of air from the world outside. It is very hard for a Princess nurtured in the hothouse of a Palace to get a true sense of values.

I had always tried to show her that Palace life was not like that which others led, and in her careful, considerate way she had listened to me.

But it was still difficult for her to realize that the mass of people's lives lay so far from hers. I thought Sir Frederick, with his broader experience, might supply just the touch I felt necessary.

And I knew that if he was anything at all like his sister he would combine charm with efficiency in a way which Princess Elizabeth would welcome.

Some time later I received a note from him. Would I kindly meet him so that he could learn a little about the character of the Princess? He had been told that I was the best person to approach, and remembering what his sister had told him about me, he looked forward to the meeting.

I replied that I would be delighted to give what information I could. But I must have hinted at the thought which Members of the Household had been puzzling about. Why should he, a man of action and ability, choose such a comparatively sedentary position?

I had a charming little letter posted from the house in Cornwall in which he and his wife, Daphne du Maurier, were living. It was dated January 10, 1948, and ended:

I do not think you need assuring that, when I was approached about being Princess Elizabeth's Comptroller, I realized very fully that I was undertaking what I consider to be the most honourable and impor-

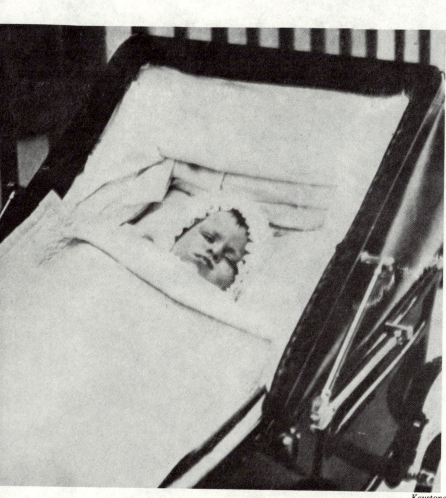

Queen Elizabeth takes an airing in the famous pram.

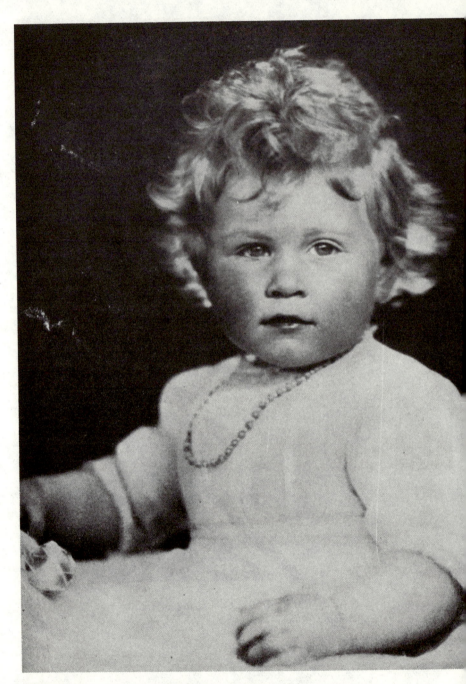

Queen Elizabeth at the age of one.

Queen Elizabeth and her mother watch
the Aldershot Tattoo, 1932.

Acm

Queen Elizabeth at thirteen.

me

Queen Elizabeth and Princess Margaret Rose enjoying their favorite sport on the Queen's fourteenth birthday.

The two Princesses on the Royal Family's tour of South Africa, 1947.

The Queen with her beloved father,
George VI, at Windsor, 1946.

Queen Elizabeth looks over her stamp collection.

Queen Elizabeth broadcasting from Capetown
to the youth of the British Empire on her
twenty-first birthday.

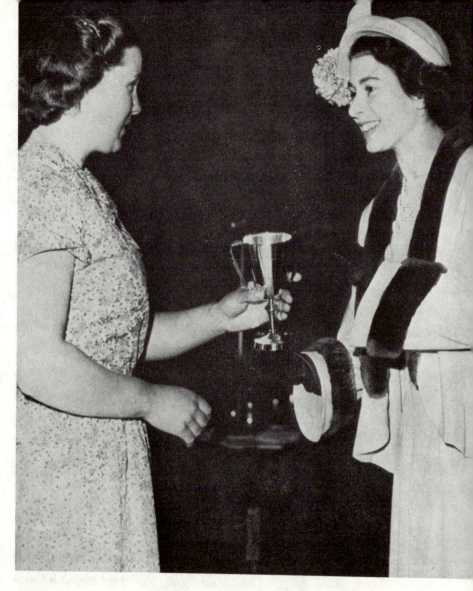

On her endless round of public duties
Queen Elizabeth awards a prize at a
Farmers' Club.

Queen Elizabeth tests a Miles driver-trainer at a Safety Exhibition.

Queen Elizabeth cheers a young patient at the Banstead hospital.

Acme

A Royal Highland Fling. The Queen dances with David
Bogle at a ball in Scotland.

Keystone

Queen Elizabeth drives her own engine at
the Swinton Locomotive Works.

Taking King George's place at the Trooping
of the Colors on the King's last birthday.

After receiving an honorary Doctor of Laws degree at London University, the Queen and her husband chat with Arthur Wint, the famous runner.

tant appointment which could be offered to anyone in
the world.

The sincerity of that paragraph made me more than
ever keen to meet him. Here was someone, I felt, who
would be coming to Princess Elizabeth full of enthusiasm for the job.

She was excited about it too. Like the rest of us, she
had been deeply moved by the heroism of those Arnhem troops. It was with some excitement, therefore,
that I waited for Sir Frederick's return to London.

I was not disappointed.

My first impression of Sir Frederick—"Boy" as I later
came to call him as do all his friends—was of a lean,
brown, intelligent face from which shone the same
bright eyes I had so admired in his sister.

I was in my room in the Palace one day when the
phone rang.

"This is Frederick Browning here," said a voice. "Can
I come and see you now? Or would you rather come
down?"

I was about to leave the Palace anyway. I thought I
would call in and see the new Comptroller in his office
along The Master of the Household's corridor, and then
make my way out of the small Police Gate which leads
into Buckingham Palace Road.

"I'll be down in a few minutes," I said.

Palace routine must be very confusing to an out-
sider thrust into it for the first time after a life spent

in other circles. But I was at once impressed by "Boy's" attitude.

He was then going through lists of servants who had applied to go with the Princess to Clarence House. It was evident that he was very much on top of the job, tackling it with a brisk and military efficiency.

"Here's an interesting thing," he told me, after we had chatted for a while. "This is a list of policemen stationed at the Palace who have applied for posts at Clarence House."

He showed me a piece of paper with a long list of names on it. I could see that he was impressed. Men do not normally volunteer to change from a post they know well to a new one which may be less comfortable, unless they have some strong personal reason.

"She must be a very delightful person," said "Boy," who had not then met the Queen more than a few times.

"You'll find she is the most wonderful person in the world," I told him.

Queen Elizabeth's kindness and consideration, which I mentioned earlier, embraces everyone she meets. I can remember her now, playing in the nursery at 145 Piccadilly, with her friend Lady Mary Cambridge.

They made a delightful pair, forming an attachment which has lasted right through the years. When we were at Windsor Castle during the war and Princess Elizabeth was chafing to be allowed to join the A.T.S.,

Lady Mary was already doing wonderful work as a nurse in the blitzed East End of London.

Princess Elizabeth would use this as a lever with which to force her argument. "Look what Mary's doing," she would say to her father. "And I am just stuck down here doing nothing."

But there was never a hint of jealousy about her. It was real admiration for Lady Mary and not envy which prompted her to use her cousin as an illustration.

In the schoolroom when they were small, they would most often play horse games, which were the Princess's favorites. But here again her thoughtfulness was very marked. The high spot of the game for each of the children was to stand in the middle of the mock circus ring, playing ringmaster and brandishing the whip which drove the "horses" round. This was a part much sought after.

But I noticed that Princess Elizabeth would voluntarily give it up when she felt she had had her share.

Queen Elizabeth's consideration was very noticeable in her attitude to servants. I read with astonishment the other day a story about her which showed her telling some tongue-tied man who was slow to answer her questions that he must speak because "it's Royalty asking."

She would never say such a thing.

It is quite foreign to her nature to impose her position in any way. Rather, she would take extra care to make sure she never wounded other people's feelings because they were not in a position to answer back.

Often, when the King and Queen were lunching away from Buckingham Palace, I would take the two girls to meals with the Household.

They enjoyed this, as they were friendly little people, and it was a change for them to see fresh faces during meals.

On these occasions Princess Elizabeth would take the head of the table in place of Sir Piers Legh, the Master of the Household, and swiftly arrange her table.

She played the part of hostess admirably, never leaving people standing about but getting them seated in the places she had already worked out for them.

She made her disposition very neatly. "You sit here, Sir Piers," she would say, pointing beside her, "and you there, Crawfie," and so on round the table.

As she sat down I would see her shoot a little glance to where the footmen stood waiting along the wall.

Sometimes there was a new footman, rather pink in the face, as it was the first time he had waited at the Royal Table. The Princess would sense this at once and knowing he was feeling embarrassed would take extra trouble to give him room to serve her properly.

When he proffered her a dish she would take it firmly and let him know she had hold of it. If the man had dropped a dish and felt humiliated, she would have been more uncomfortable than he.

Then, as the man left the room on some errand, she

would ask Sir Piers about him, find out a little of his background and what jobs he had held before. In this way the staff became to her not mere automatons, but human beings, each with a separate individuality.

They felt this and were deeply grateful to her.

Her sympathy extended equally to animals. She would take endless trouble to see that the dogs were properly fed, for example. The Corgis, Susan and Jane, used to sleep in her room at the Palace. Feeding them was quite a ritual.

Promptly at five o'clock a footman would approach along the corridor carrying a large checked cloth which he would lay down on the boards between the wall and the carpet.

Then he would put down the two separate bowls of food and drink and knock on the Princess's door to let her know the dogs' dinner was there.

She would then come out and mix it for them herself —standing by to see they did not eat it too quickly.

If it was raining while she was taking them for a walk, she would be most careful to see they were dried properly, treating them as carefully as babies.

Sometimes Princess Margaret would have taken them out in the rain. Then Princess Elizabeth would inspect them to make sure they were quite dry.

"Did you dry the dogs, Margaret?" she would ask. And the younger Princess, in a voice of indignant innocence, would say, "Of *course* I did."

Then would come Princess Elizabeth's voice, very

shrill. "You couldn't have done! The towel is absolutely spotless," and she would rub them again herself.

The elevators at Buckingham Palace are very old and ponderous. They move slowly. But they are carefully looked after by two engineers.

Princess Elizabeth would always make sure that the dogs were kept far from the gates in case they got their tails or noses jammed. "Come here, Susan," she would say. "Keep still or you'll lose an ear."

When a bomb fell on Hampton Court in 1941, where the Royal horses had been evacuated, one of the carriage horses in the stables was injured and was sent down to Windsor Castle to recuperate.

The veterinary surgeon who had to operate on the animal asked us if we'd like to see it. The Princesses were very excited, and one day after lunch we all trooped out to inspect the invalid.

He was a large horse looking quite fit except for two gashes in his side where the splinters had torn holes in the flesh.

Princess Elizabeth was greatly concerned. "Oh, the poor thing!" she said, and wanted to know if there was anything she could do to help. "Is he quite comfortable?" she asked. "Can he lie down to sleep? Or does it hurt him too much?"

The veterinary made a good job and the wounds healed splendidly. But it was a long time before Princess Elizabeth lost her look of concern when anyone mentioned the horse.

This interest of hers in animals was not confined to horses and dogs. Lord Louis Mountbatten came back on leave during the war bringing as a present a large, scaly lizard which we learned was a chameleon.

Princess Elizabeth was thrilled and quickly had a box made in which to keep the creature. Princess Margaret rushed off and got a copy of Debrett on which we put him. He immediately changed to red.

I have a horror of all slimy, crawly things. When the King was still Duke of York he took us all to the Zoo, where one of the Keepers showed us behind the scenes at the Reptile House.

He brought out a very sleepy, sinuous python to show us which coiled itself lazily round him. I can still feel the horror I felt then. I was glad to see the others also turn a little pale, though they kept their courage under better control than I did.

The Princesses assured me that the chameleon was not at all like that. "Just touch him, Crawfie," they urged. "Just put your finger on him. He's warm as anything and quite dry."

Princess Elizabeth used to carry him on a hand to the big windows in the dining room where there were always a few bluebottles buzzing round. Here she would hold the creature in a convenient position so that its long black tongue could snake out and seize one of these unfortunate flies.

She was so insistent that I finally forced myself to feel his scaly back. They were quite right. He was warm and dry, but still not at all the sort of pet I should have chosen myself.

I was very grateful that they were both kind-hearted little girls and not the sort who would have put him in my bed.

With Princess Elizabeth, at least, I had the feeling she would refrain from such tricks, as much out of consideration for the chameleon as for me.

Eventually it sickened and its beady little eyes grew less bright. The Princesses were desolate. In the end I found a gatekeeper who had lived in the tropics and said he knew something about looking after chameleons, so we handed the creature into his care.

For a time it throve. Then one day the gatekeeper reported it dead. Princess Elizabeth was very sad. "We must bury him in proper state," she said.

The gatekeeper gave us a little white box about a foot long. It was sealed up at either end with a red seal, and looked rather like a package from the druggist.

Then the three of us marched into the gardens to find a suitable cemetery. We had not gone far when Princess Elizabeth stopped with a look of horror on her face.

"But how do we *know* he's dead?" she asked.

Then we had to undo the coffin and make sure. There was no doubt about it, so we buried him under a flowering shrub and Princess Elizabeth hummed a hymn tune.

In my time at the Palace, Princess Elizabeth's secretary was Mr. John Colville, known to everyone as Jock. He is a very brilliant young man who was on Winston

Churchill's staff during the early part of the war, before he insisted on joining the R.A.F.

Each day Jock would drive to the Palace from his mother's charming little house in Mulberry Walk, Chelsea, and go through the Princess's correspondence.

He had an office just along the passage from the Princess's rooms, to which he would be summoned when she was ready to read her letters.

It is a popular misconception that Royalty are surrounded by Advisers—men appointed with the sole object of guiding them through all the moves of their lives.

This is not so. This Royal Family, at least, have very firm ideas of their own about what they are going to do. But naturally they do depend on their secretaries to advise them about things outside their experience.

In this way Princess Elizabeth will go through the many, many requests she gets—to open this bazaar, or name that ship—and pick the ones she thinks most worthy out of a thousand-and-one requests.

It is her secretary's job to make sure that she does not pick the one which for some reason might start one of those wrangles which occur when people of prejudice feel they have been slighted.

For example, Royalty have to be careful what connection they have with religious organizations outside the Church of England of which the King is officially the temporal head.

It is here that the secretary's knowledge is so valu-

able. He can say, "Ma'am, I think it would be better
to refuse that offer. If you accept, there might be some
hard feelings among so and so. . . ."

In this respect only can the secretary be called an
adviser.

I remember feeling very sorry for both Jock and
"Boy" Browning when they were publicly taken to
task by a certain newspaper for "allowing" Princess
Elizabeth to make too many engagements so soon after
the birth of Princess Anne.

I sympathize with the secretary and the Comptroller
because Queen Elizabeth is a reasonable person in all
save one direction: she will not listen to pleas to spare
herself.

It is hard to convey the truth about Royalty's passion
for duty.

I remember once when Princess Elizabeth was still
in her teens she woke one day feeling very ill indeed.
But it was all I could do to persuade her to stay in bed.

"I must not take the easy way out, Crawfie," she kept
insisting, and this while she had a temperature which
would have put most people out of action for two or
three days.

This is a fair example of what her secretary and
Comptroller have to deal with. Jock came to me one
day to complain: "Crawfie, I wish you'd speak to the
Princess. She *will* take on such an enormous program.
She won't listen to me when I tell her she is working

too hard. She just says, 'Jock, I can't disappoint all those people.'"

I told him there was little I could do. I always found Princess Elizabeth most amenable if I were appealing to her on behalf of someone else. But if I approached her about herself, she would brush my protests aside.

"I've just got to do it, Crawfie," she would say. "After all, it's my job."

"Crawfie," Princess Elizabeth said to me just before she left to inspect the Grenadier Guards whose Commander in Chief she had just become at the age of sixteen, "I've got such a fluttering feeling inside."

But she never let her "nerves" affect her performance at public functions.

Do people ever ask themselves, on seeing Queen Elizabeth going smoothly and gracefully about her duties at a public function, whether she has ever overcome the handicap of shyness which so often afflicts Royalty as well as ordinary folk?

She was not a shy child, running away when people spoke to her, but was always ready to stand up and meet people.

I remember the King saying to me once, as we watched her strut on the stage (built in Queen Victoria's time and still hung with the dark purple gold-bordered heavy curtains that had screened the Victorian tableaux of so many years ago) at Windsor Castle for one of our pantomimes: "Where does she get her poise? I was always terrified of getting up in public."

I am sure that Princess Elizabeth enjoyed most of the functions she attended. And she lets others share her pleasure. The fact is that she likes people, is interested in them and the way they live.

There is a great deal of organization needed for a Royal visit. There is tremendous advance excitement and detailed preparation. All the local dignitaries get out their robes or have their best suits pressed. Their wives are thrown into a frenzy of ironing and other activity.

Those responsible for the ceremonies of the occasion are busy too. Precedence of presentation to Royalty is a matter of great importance to them.

If the Princess was to arrive by train there was an official welcome to prepare, police arrangements to be made at the station, and then the planning of a day packed with visits, speeches, and drives.

This was a day of days for the town and its citizens; but for the Princess this was her life, day after day. She can look forward to a future of similar functions; the trip by train or car; the loyal speech of welcome: her gracious reply—everything falling into a set and familiar pattern. Local newspapers filled their columns with descriptions of her smile, her voice, the names of people who had been presented to her, the decorations in the streets, the crowds.

Local photographers dressed their shopwindows with

pictures showing the Princess walking beside the Mayor or the Bishop, or accepting a bouquet from a schoolboy.

For every one of the many thousands who flock to see her the visit of a Queen is a great occasion. For those who are fortunate enough to be on the platform or in the same room or garden with her, it is an unforgettable experience, to be treasured all their lives.

Unforgettable for them! But what of her, who must be somewhere else tomorrow, walking the aisles of another cathedral, listening to the Dean's reminiscences, inspecting more walls filled with paintings, and making bright and memorable remarks about them?

Surely the wonder is that she remembers any of the hundreds of people she meets in a week of such visits.

But she does remember. To keep names and faces in her mind is an important part of her task. And her memory starts working even before she comes to a place.

This may be her first visit to the town, but she knows that her father or her grandfather visited it long ago. Perhaps he received a gold casket or some other memento.

Memento is for memory, and Queen Elizabeth is careful to recall the gift in reply to the Lord Mayor's loyal address. She knows his name and the names of other local notabilities who may be presented to her. And she will recall their names and faces if ever they come before her again.

Conscious memory training could have been responsible for some of this, although as Governess to the Princess I must confess that I made no concentrated effort in that direction. It is part of her heritage, part of the tradition of graciousness that has been handed down to her with her royal birthright.

But even an inherited faculty has to be nurtured by hard work, and that is something Queen Elizabeth was never afraid of, even as a child. Busy men may forget names and faces, but a British Queen, as busy as anyone, allows herself no such latitude.

No one who has seen her on one of these visits has felt for a moment that it was just routine for her. Because it was not so, really. It was meeting people—and she likes people.

She always has. I have seen her stand for hours at the window of her apartment in Buckingham Palace from which she could see, through the lace curtains, Big Ben's face and look right down the Mall to the Admiralty Arch. Then she would look down to the scattered sight-seers in front of the Palace gates. They would look up, asking one another which room is the King's, where the Throne room is, trying to imagine what is behind each window.

They little thought that at the same time a Royal Princess was wondering about them!

It was the same in Canada, where Princess Elizabeth was undertaking the first State visit of her career, as the representative of her father.

To the King and Queen at home the daily news of

the progress of their daughter's tour of the Dominion must have recalled vivid memories of their own visit to Canada and the United States in the summer of July, 1939, just before the outbreak of war.

Queen Elizabeth knew for fifteen years the dignity and responsibility that the Heir to the Throne must carry.

Naturally, a child could not at once appreciate that her life thenceforth would be very different from that which she had enjoyed and expected to go on enjoying.

At moments a serious look came into her face. Although she could not have realized then all that the change would mean to her, she certainly did know that in leaving the old home at 145 Piccadilly, after the Abdication, she would be leaving some of her childhood behind.

She was no plaster saint, but always a very human little person—sometimes quick-tempered and inclined to be a little overcritical. The curious thing, however, was that she was quick to see her own faults when they were pointed out to her, and eager to correct them.

Her heritage and the knowledge she had of it called on her to set a high standard for herself. I do not think I have ever met a more resolute person, of any age.

With her beauty and intelligence, if she had been born into an undistinguished family, she could have won distinction for herself in any work she undertook.

The same purpose which I always admired in her has

enabled her to mold herself into the work that she has been called upon to do.

As a child she would always listen to reason, and knew reason when she saw it. Like every intelligent child, she would ask "Why?" but, unlike many, she would always accept a logical answer.

Seeing her later so perfectly dressed, whether for a military parade or for a garden party, it seemed strange to me to recall that in her teens she was never particularly concerned about her appearance. But since wearing the right things at the right times was a duty, she conformed without demur.

At one time she had a great deal of fun experimenting with various styles of make-up. One day she came down with a vivid splotch of crimson caked round her lips. This apparition in the sober surroundings of our schoolroom at Windsor Castle was as startling a splash of red as a poppy in the snow.

She saw me looking rather dubiously at her, but pretended to take no notice.

At last she could contain herself no longer. "Crawfie," she exclaimed, "what is the matter with you this morning? Why have you been staring at me?"

"It's your mouth," I said firmly. "You look as if you'd dipped it into a pot of plum jam. It doesn't go with your coloring at all. You need a light cheery lipstick."

Nothing more was said. She did not wipe the paint off at once, but before the end of the morning the smear had become a little less obvious.

As the days passed, she lightened the shade and shaped it to the pleasant lines of her own mouth. Princess Elizabeth, like many other young girls, lived and learned, but she learned faster than most.

One of the first things that one must realize about a Princess is that it is not truly a position but a vocation, a calling. She had been dedicated to it rather than trained for it in the ordinary sense of training.

Part Four

EVERY Sunday morning at the Royal Lodge, Windsor, there was an unvarying routine. At ten minutes to eleven the Royal Family and I would gather in the hall, together with those guests who happened to be staying with them, and walk the forty yards or more to the little chapel in the Park.

The Royal Family had a private pew curtained in such a manner that the congregation could see only their profiles while they were standing. On the Sunday morning I am thinking of there was a visiting preacher.

The resident Vicar was then the Rev. Francis Stone, a most cultured man. He was a fine-looking man who gave great distinction to the little chapel.

The visiting preacher was a short, stout man with a

shining bald head. He had been delivering his sermon for some minutes when I saw a bee approach him in a wary circle.

It flew round him several times, getting nearer with each circuit. I watched it, fascinated, to see where it would settle. Awful pictures of it stinging him rose to my mind, and I saw from the look I stole at the King, sitting on my left in front of me, that similar thoughts were passing through his mind.

The low drone formed a sort of background to the sermon which I had now quite forgotten in the excitement of watching the bee's narrowing spiral which finally came to its apex in a neat landing right in the center of the bald patch of the preacher's head.

I gave a sort of strangled cough and quickly buried my face in my handkerchief. But before I did so I caught sight of Princess Elizabeth, then about ten years of age. Her face was set firm and calm.

I knew she had been watching with the same fascination as I; but she had already achieved an iron control of her emotions, and all I could see was that the flowers on her hat were quivering with her suppressed laughter.

This control is a noticeable faculty in the Royal Family. In private life they laugh very readily. When George, my husband, first came to the Palace and the Princesses were with me, he was struck by the amount of laughing we did—not at him, of course, or at anybody else, but among ourselves. We seemed such a happy trio, he thought.

Through the years little jokes had grown among us. Princess Margaret had only to say, "D'you remember the day when . . ." to set us off.

Princess Elizabeth used to laugh very often. I loved to hear her musical, tinkling voice break into an uncontrollable giggle when she was small.

But unlike other children with a strong sense of humor, she had to learn to curb it at times, to stifle it almost, from a very early age. What can be excused in an ordinary child and attributed to youth might cause a great deal of surprise coming from a Princess.

But sometimes situations occurred, like that of the bee, which were so ludicrous that she had to make an obvious effort to suppress the impulse to laugh. I know how difficult this is to do as I, too, had to learn to control such impulses.

One of the first things which impressed me about the Royal Family when I joined them was their really genuine love of laughter. In those days King George was very boyish and would sometimes laugh in an uninhibited and refreshing way for several minutes at a good joke.

They were always a very jolly family, and while they were playing together it was wonderful to see the gusto with which the King entered into the children's games. To me, he was the ideal father.

That was in their private life. But on more dignified

occasions they have a remarkable control over their sense of humor.

On one occasion the Royal Family were entertaining a lady who, I could see, was somewhat embarrassed. She was a large woman, wearing a most peculiar hat which I knew had already caught the Princess's eyes.

She lowered herself into a rather flimsy chair which, to the accompaniment of splintering wood, promptly buckled and collapsed under her.

There are few things funnier to behold—from the onlooker's point of view. But not a flicker of a smile appeared on any of our faces. Not only because of our strict training, but because we were all overwhelmed with sympathy that such an accident should have happened.

To Their Majesties, the King and Queen, and to the Princess, nothing was funny to them when it caused pain and embarrassment to others.

That was just one occasion on which their control had to be exercised to avoid hurting people's feelings. But we would not have been human if we had not seen the funny side of the incident and laughed wholeheartedly about it when we were alone and the lady had gone.

Before I had been very long with the Royal Family, I had learned to control my impulse to giggle at the wrong moment. I had learned to play tricks with my mind, to fix it on a certain point, to shut out the remark which I knew was going to be extremely funny, to avoid looking at the man whose mustaches wobbled about as if they were going to drop off, and to drug my mind by repeating long passages of poetry.

But before I learned such tricks, I was not always so discreet as I might have been.

I often think now of a make-believe game that the Princesses, especially Princess Margaret, were fond of playing when they were children. We called it "*If*."

Princess Margaret would prance about the playroom chanting, "If I could be anything I liked, Crawfie, do you know what I'd be?"

"A good girl, I should think," I would reply. "Certainly a Princess should be good."

"But if I weren't a Princess, Crawfie, I should like to be . . ."

And she would search her lively imagination for a dozen fantastic professions, some of which she had read about in books and others that she had invented on the spot. Her images were always colorful and stimulating. She was a very nimble-minded little girl.

Princess Elizabeth sometimes entered the game, but she always took it very seriously, and tried to connect it with the real life outside, of which she could catch only glimpses. She was absorbed by healthy curiosity about the way other people lived, and tried to put herself in their places. Instead of playing a game, she exercised this faculty while we drove in the streets or in the country.

Among the little throng always to be seen waiting outside the Palace were several familiar faces. Many elderly women were among them.

"We know them, don't we, Crawfie?" Princess Elizabeth would say. "But still, I wonder who they are?"

There was one old lady, dressed in black, with a lean, sad face, who was always waiting at Hyde Park Corner at four o'clock on Friday afternoons as we drove down from the Palace to the Royal Lodge, Windsor.

We always took the same route—up Constitution Hill, and round the traffic island into the Park. The Princesses became very much interested in her, speculating on whether she would be there or not.

She always was.

As our car came abreast of the gate where the traffic has to slow down in order to file through the arches into the Park, there she would be, watching and waiting.

We used to wonder what happened to her during the summer, when we were at Balmoral. Did she read of the Royal movements in the newspapers and plan her life accordingly?

Princess Elizabeth would be very worried about her if we were ever delayed on our journey, or—as rarely happened—there was a change in our week-end routine.

"I hope she will not wait too long," the Princess would say. "She doesn't look very strong."

She was always interested in the "outside world" on which she considered me an authority—although to tell the truth I saw very little of it—and would ask me endless questions about it. But I believe that until her marriage the Princess had no very clear understanding of the way people lived outside palace walls.

I would sometimes play the *"If"* game myself. What would Princess Elizabeth like to be and do, I often asked myself, "if" she were free to choose? My interest was intensified by the fact that she was planning her own first household while I was planning mine.

The course of her life was set. Certain things happened, always had happened, and always would continue to happen so far as she knew. A child does not ask what water tastes like, or puzzle over the way she breathes. These things are taken for granted. So, then, was Princess Elizabeth's way of living.

But on her honeymoon, and certainly afterward, when she flew to visit Prince Philip in Malta, Princess Elizabeth saw and experienced for the first time the life of an ordinary girl not living in a palace.

She could never be quite free from all attention, of course, however thoughtful people are. And in Malta the citizens made a genuine effort not to cloud her visit with the kind of staring attention she gets nearly everywhere else.

But Princess Elizabeth could never dissolve into the background and enjoy herself as an unknown person can, although on certain rare occasions she has seen what life might be like if she had not been a Princess.

As I think over her personality, trying to settle on

those points which seem to me on reflection most characteristic, I find one word rising continually in my mind: thoughtfulness.

Let us suppose that she had been plain Miss Elizabeth Windsor. What then? How would she have differed?

After careful thought the only difference I think which would have been obvious in her would be a slightly less serious outlook on life.

Princess Elizabeth never had the gay, carefree character of Princess Margaret. The two girls of the same birth and upbringing differ in many ways. Their complexions are different, for example.

Princess Margaret has an excellent skin, but not of the same alabaster quality as Queen Elizabeth's. In summer Princess Margaret gets quite sunburned, as I do.

We used to joke and say that the heat of the passing busses was enough to give us a tan. Queen Elizabeth and her mother have skin of a similar type and they both have to guard not only against tanning but also against sunburn.

The complexions of both Princesses were an agreeable surprise to Margaret Truman, the President's daughter, when she visited Great Britain.

"One wouldn't know from photographs alone," she said, "how pretty the Princesses really are. Princess Elizabeth's skin is a dream."

Though Queen Elizabeth had little of her sister's

lighthearted way, she was not solemn. You can see that she always thinks deeply about things, takes others' suffering to heart, and is careful never to say anything that might hurt. That is so much her that no different upbringing could change it.

But relieved of the load of responsibility she had to bear all through her adolescence, when the whole attention of other girls was directed toward the careers they had chosen, enjoying themselves, or choosing their husbands—she might have been freer to indulge her really remarkable sense of humor.

It was not hard, then, to visualize Queen Elizabeth as Mrs. Mountbatten, being a very amusing and entertaining sort of person, easy to please, ready to laugh, but invariably considerate of the feelings of others.

Queen Elizabeth loves the countryside, particularly the soft woods round the Royal Lodge, Windsor. Were she free, I think she would most like to live in that part of the country, with perhaps a house in town.

She is very fond of the theater, and though country life is her favorite, I know she would be miserable if she were to be cut off from just that sense of excitement about the theater which fascinates me.

I see her as an excellent housewife and mother. Whatever she does, she does well. Though she has no natural aptitude for knitting and sewing, were it ever really necessary for her to master their technique, I know she would settle down industriously to do so.

Dogs and horses would form a large part of her life,

just as they do now. She would be most happy with a stable full of horses, for she is very knowledgeable about them.

Her house would be a happy one, for she has that warm-hearted temperament which makes all around her feel content. Her servants would be well-cared for and would certainly love her.

Though Queen Elizabeth can be very firm if she feels she is being taken advantage of, she is a kind and considerate employer.

Were this miraculous change of status to occur overnight, were she to find herself suddenly just an ordinary citizen, there would be a great number of adjustments she would have to make.

I noticed when I left the Palace that in many ways I was quite unused to the hurly-burly of modern life. I had come straight from the comparatively quiet town of Dunfermline to a life in London which was in no way typical of the lives my friends were leading.

When Royalty go anywhere, the route is planned, they are driven by trained chauffeurs, and the police are warned beforehand to see that everything goes smoothly.

In this way, the Royal Family never come to grips with the perilous business of crossing streets or fighting their way into underground trains or onto busses.

I am afraid I was the same. When I lived at 145 Piccadilly, I used always to take a taxi to whatever destination I was bound for in my own time: at the Palace

I was provided with a Royal car which took me and my luggage to the station when I was going home for my holiday. I never really encountered the problem of traffic at all.

Crossing roads was another problem. For the Royal Family the police clear a way. If they walk, traffic is diverted.

In this way they never learn to "Look Left!" or do any of the other precautionary reconnoitering which becomes second nature to ordinary travelers.

Nor did I. I still find that if I want to get to the other side of the road, I just step off the pavement in a direction which will take me there in the shortest possible time.

Queen Elizabeth would find the same problem were she thrust into normal life. One does not know, in the quiet seclusion of a palace, how very terrifying one's fellow citizens become once they are behind a steering wheel.

Queen Elizabeth loves children. Many times as we drove round London on our way to and from those Monday-afternoon treats Queen Mary used to give us, or on the way down to the Royal Lodge, Windsor, she would suddenly lean forward and say, "Look, what a lovely little girl that is." Or, "Isn't he a sweet-looking child?"

Whenever she had to speak with children or take

bouquets from their embarrassed hands, a new gentleness came over her.

"Thank you so much," she would say, smiling at them in a pleasant, open way which made them feel that here was not some magnificent lady, but a kind elder sister or aunt. She has a way with children which is quite delightful to watch. Obviously she loves to be with them.

That is very evident with her own children.

We used to play, I remember, a game of peep-bo together when she was small. The Princess would be playing in the gardens behind 145 Piccadilly, and I would hide myself behind a bush.

Suddenly I would pop my head out and say "Peep-bo," at which she would go off into a long gurgle of laughter, which I would stimulate again by repeating the performance whenever it seemed likely to stop. It was a game of which she never tired.

I was amused the other day to see a charming picture of her taken at Clarence House, where she was obviously playing just the same game with Prince Charles.

There is nothing artificial about Queen Elizabeth. If she plays a game with children, she is not just "playing down to them." She enjoys it as much as they. She has the priceless gift of being able to forget herself and her surroundings while doing anything which interests her.

This love of children makes her a very human person. I know that the time she has to give to her official

H. R. H. Philip, Duke of Edinburgh, the Queen's husband.

The Queen and Prince Philip during their honeymoon.

The Queen and the Duke of Edinburgh in the Throne Room of Buckingham Palace after their marriage.

Queen Elizabeth and her husband at Broadlands, Ramsey.

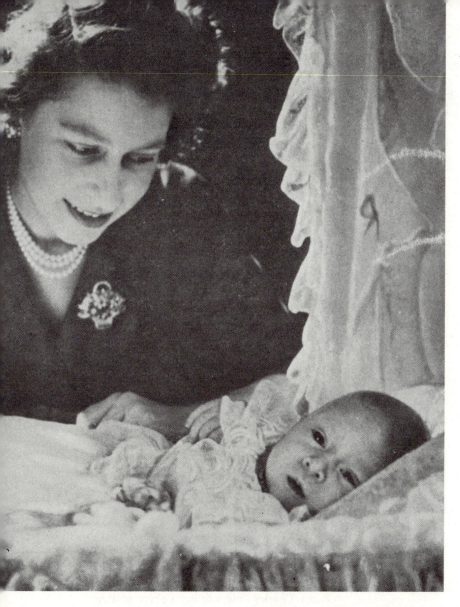

The Queen and her one-month-old first
child, Prince Charles.

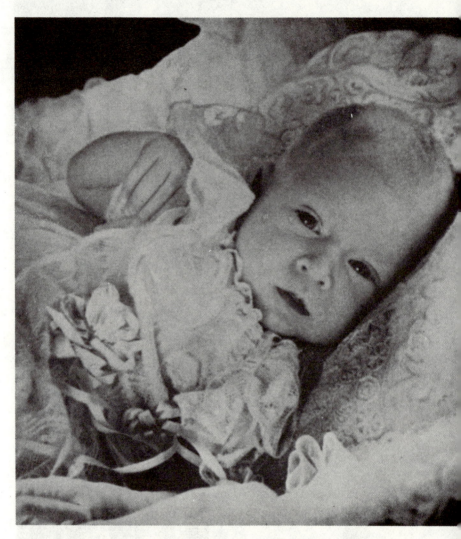

Prince Charles Philip Arthur George of Edinburgh, aged one month.

The christening of Princess Anne Elizabeth Alice Louise. King George VI and the Duke of Edinburgh stand behind, while Queen Elizabeth holds her baby daughter between her grandmother Queen Mary and the Queen Mother, holding Prince Charles.

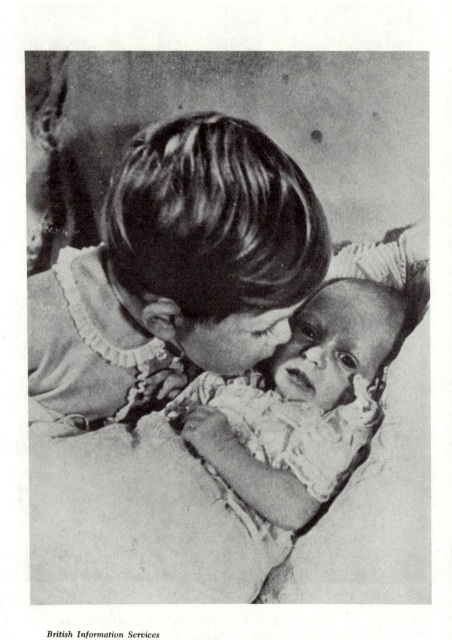

Prince Charles kisses his new baby sister.

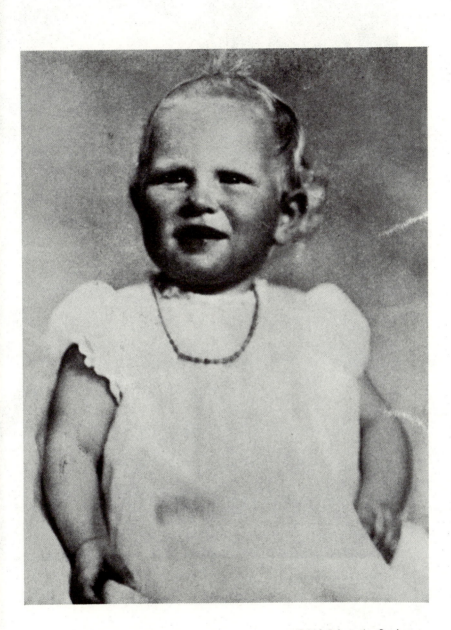

Princess Anne, one year old, on August 15, 1951.

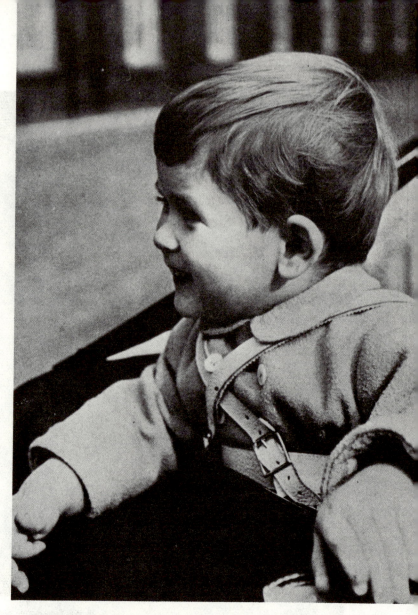

Prince Charles at the age of two.

Queen Elizabeth and her children.

King George VI and his grandson.

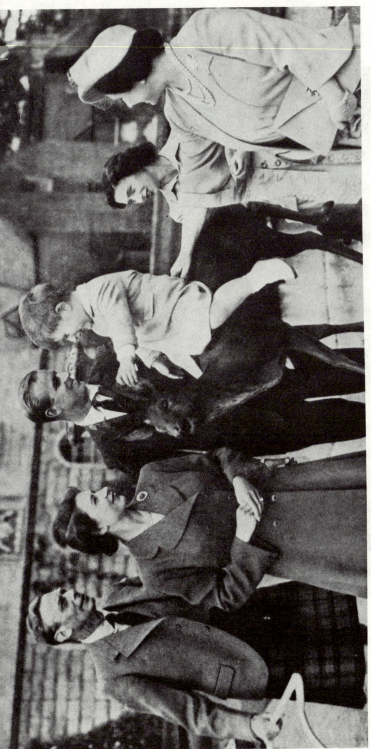

The Royal Family on holiday at Balmoral Castle, Scotland.

Queen Elizabeth and her family.

Prince Charles on his third birthday, November 14, 1951.

Marcus Adams—Keystone

Her Majesty, Queen Elizabeth II. Her latest portrait.

duties and the many calls she has upon her day make each moment she spends with Prince Charles and Princess Anne precious to her.

As a private citizen she would be able to spend most of her day with them, and very lucky children they would be.

This thought brings to mind the touching reunion between her and Prince Charles on her return from Malta, where she had visited her husband.

At the airport a silver aircraft touched down on the runway, slowed to a stop, and then swept in a graceful arc toward the control tower.

The crowd which had waited surged forward, surrounding the plane, while panting policemen struggled to keep them from crushing the tiny figure in a lemon-colored coat, clutching his nannie's hand, and staring with round eyes at the now-stationary airplane.

The aircraft's door opened. A member of the crew came down the steps toward the child and said a few words to his nannie. Then he lifted the little boy into the aircraft.

Mother and child, together for the first time in eleven weeks, embraced in the plane, while the crowd waited patiently. And none among them grudged Princess Elizabeth the enjoyment of a few precious moments of privacy before she stepped out to acknowledge the cheers.

A very pretty picture comes to my mind of the house Queen Elizabeth might choose to live in if she had her way. I see it set within very old and mellow walls, with perhaps peaches and pears growing along the south face.

The house would be Georgian, small and square, with a sense of intimacy about it which one always misses in a palace.

It would have gay curtains and light, airy rooms. There would be flowers everywhere, for Queen Elizabeth loves to come into a house filled with their inviting scents.

The kitchen would be bright and shining, just as the kitchens are at Clarence House, and visitors would be made abundantly welcome.

Queen Elizabeth has always had a way of making people feel comfortable and at their ease all her life. It springs from her desire that everyone around her must be made happy, and has nothing whatever to do with her position. It is part of her nature, as are so many of her other outstanding qualities.

I can never say often enough that it takes no effort to write of Queen Elizabeth's charm, her kindliness and consideration, for those are graven in her character.

I noticed them in her from the very first time we met when she was only six, and I traced them through the seventeen years we spent together until I saw them ripen into the really delightful mature personality which is hers now.

It is not her Royalty which makes Queen Elizabeth regal: it is herself.

Queen Elizabeth, mistress of her own household, with her own family around her, and carrying the responsibilities of the Throne is very much her father's daughter.

Throughout the long association with the Royal Family which I have been privileged to enjoy, I have constantly had before me her parents' example of perfect unity. The King, the Queen, and their two lovely daughters always took such pleasure in one another's company that they seemed to draw strength from one another, and so had no need of other support.

Their harmony gave no scope to the traditional jealousy of courtiers. There was none of the court favoritism and petty bickering of the old times, for there was no chance for jealousies to arise. The Royal Family as an indivisible unit, bound together by love and loyalty, stood above and apart from all that.

It is as indivisible as ever now that Princess Elizabeth is Queen.

During the King's illness and the absence of the Duke of Edinburgh in Malta, the Princess and her mother were almost constant companions. It was not only her deep love and sympathy for her mother that kept her by her side, but also her responsibilities as the King's daughter.

And there was in that companionship also a continuing of the good habits that have grown up with her from childhood. When Princess Elizabeth and Princess

Margaret were children it was their father's greatest delight to romp and play with them.

From the very first I felt that there was something special about his feeling for Princess Elizabeth. He showed it in a different way from his obvious love for Princess Margaret, who could always charm him.

Princess Margaret's personality was so compelling that she could make him snuggle up and tell stories when he really was too tired.

But Princess Elizabeth would always sense his mood and conform to it. When I used to see them walk together from the Royal Lodge to the stables, where they fed the horses, they seemed to me a perfect picture of father and daughter.

The King, so tall and slim, bending slightly to the little figure by his side—and she, with her hand confidently holding his, always had so much to talk about. And so seriously.

They never seemed to be exchanging mere childish pleasantries. To Princess Elizabeth he always used his normal, adult tone, as one understanding, sensible person to another.

Princess Elizabeth responded eagerly to such treatment, and loved to be taken seriously. She wanted to hear what was going on, and to ask him questions. It was as if even then, long before her great destiny was clear before her, her inborn nature was preparing her for it.

For remember that no one could think of her then as

the future Queen of England, but only as a charming little girl, who, if certain unpredictable events came to pass, might one day be Queen. These events, not only unpredictable but unprecedented, did come to pass in less than a year—and then we were all in Buckingham Palace instead of 145 Piccadilly.

The King and Queen had less time then to romp with their daughters, who often sighed for the old days.

"I do wish Papa hadn't to see all those people," Princess Elizabeth would say. "I think it would do him good to play with us for a bit." No truer word was ever spoken. Indeed it would have done him a great deal of good.

Neither the King nor the Queen wished the Princesses to grow up to be athletic women. Of course they learned to ride and swim, but feminine ideals were always held up to them.

Their mother, particularly, was always insistent on their behaving "nicely." Not that they ever behaved otherwise; but even Royal children are apt to forget their manners when there is excitement about.

I never went to children's parties with them. A collection of excited children all demonstrating how wonderful they are, egged on by their admiring nannies and governesses, is my idea of purgatory.

Instead, Alah, their "nannie," would prepare them for the treat and bring them along for inspection. Their mother was always very firm before they set out.

"Now, darlings," she would say, "*do* be good. And be

sure and say 'thank you' very nicely before you leave. You won't forget, will you?"

And both little girls would nod their heads and promise.

Queen Elizabeth always had that natural tact and sense of good manners which carried her through. Even as quite a tiny girl she was seldom even thoughtlessly rude. She would make Princess Margaret her special charge.

"Margaret almost forgot to say 'thank you,' Crawfie," she would tell me afterward, "but I gave her a nudge, and she said it beautifully."

Until the time we moved to the Palace the girls had a normal, simple upbringing. People are continually amazed when they learn how really natural the Royal Family are. They are expected to live always in an aura of glamour and be surrounded by hundreds of bowing flunkies. This is not so.

Few families were as well-balanced. But with the host of new duties that thrust themselves upon him, the King was forced to break away a little from the close intimacy with his children.

They were a little sad to find their rooms at the Palace so far from their parents', but their mother comforted them by saying, "After all, darlings, we are only just along the passage and down some stairs. And look at the space you have to ride your horses in!"

This was a great consolation. Almost the first thing

they did, even before they had their hats off, was to decide the disposition of their horses.

Princess Elizabeth began to notice the great change forcing into their lives. "I wish Papa was here," she would say. Or, "Let's find Papa and tell him . . ."

Then she would break off. "Oh, dear, I suppose he's busy," she would end sadly.

But all this was forgotten at week ends. Every week end before the war we would go down to the Royal Lodge, the luggage ahead of us in the Palace station wagon, and the five of us following behind in one of the Royal cars.

I am easily carsick and particularly susceptible to the smooth, dignified, humming progression of the Royal cars. After King George came to the Throne there was always a detective on the box beside the chauffeur. But while he was still Duke of York we would sometimes go down unescorted.

Then I would say, "Would you mind, sir, if I sat in front with the chauffeur? I always feel that the car sways less in the front seat, and I think I shall feel better there."

This always amused the King, though he was always sympathetic to anyone's weakness. "Crawfie is surely the only person I know," he would say, "who would rather travel on the box with the chauffeur than with us."

Then I would ride with a side window slightly open and fix my mind very firmly on something else. But often when we reached the gates of Windsor Great Park I would ask the driver to stop, and I would walk the rest of the way breathing deeply to get over my queasiness.

How fortunate it was for Queen Elizabeth and Princess Margaret that neither was an only child! The sight of the two sisters enjoying each other's company and that of their parents' made me regret my own lonely childhood. When I was just one year old my father took my mother, my brother Andrew, and myself out to New Zealand, where he hoped to make a better living than in Britain.

But we had not been there long before my father was killed. Mother brought us back to Scotland to a house near a village called Gatehead in Ayrshire, on the banks of the river Irvine.

My brother Andrew is several years older than I am, and I was left very much alone. I would wander through the fields round the house amusing myself by watching the birds and listening for that little underworld of mice and rabbits which goes on beside and below the human world.

At the foot of the garden there was an old stone bridge spanning the river Irvine. I was not fond of the Irvine. It was a sluggish stream in those days, dirty gray in color and often smelling not too sweetly. Now, I am told, it is quite clean and one of the best fishing rivers in Scotland.

I never liked that bridge either. I used to cross it

several times a day on my way to the farm. I had a
little chicken which used to follow me everywhere. On
the way a huge, unfriendly bull used to bellow at us
over a hedge. At the farm I would play with the little
lambs until they grew too big and took to butting me.

I don't know how it began, but the bridge always
frightened me. One day I heard my mother talking with
a friend. This was during World War I and everyone
was very full of German atrocity stories.

My mother pointed her arm to illustrate something
she was saying about the Germans. Her finger indicated
the bridge. I don't remember the exact sense of her
words, but it gave me a most uncomfortable feeling.

In the confused way children sometimes have, from
that moment I associated the bridge with Germans. I
didn't know what or who Germans were, but I knew
that a band of them lurked below the arch. And I
would not have gone there for a million pounds.

As I look back it seems to me that such morbid feelings would never have been allowed to grow in me if I
had had some children of my own age to play with.

I was always struck by the easy, amiable way of the
two Princesses. They were never afraid or shy of people, but always went out to them in a very open and
heart-warming way.

But I think they did miss the company of a brother.
Sometimes the two Harewood boys would come, or
more often their cousins John and Andrew Elphinstone.
Then there was great delight.

Both the Elphinstones were excellent mimics, and very full of boyish tricks. The little girls thought they were wonderful.

"I do wish we had a brother," Princess Elizabeth would sigh. Then she would make me tell her about Andrew, my brother.

"Brothers have their drawbacks," I would point out diplomatically.

"But how, how, Crawfie?" she would insist. "What do you mean, *drawbacks?*"

"Well," I would answer, "they're inclined to be rough. And they tease a lot."

But nothing I could say would persuade her that a brother was not a wonderful possession.

They remained interested in the strange ways of boys and would ask me in a wondering way why so and so said that. Or why did so and so suddenly start climbing a tree in the middle of tea? I wasn't able to help them much.

One afternoon, much later, Princess Elizabeth came into my room at the Palace. It was shortly after her own marriage. George, my husband, was at the time staying in a hotel in South Kensington, while we waited for Nottingham Cottage to be made ready.

After we were married, and I was still in my rooms at the Palace, my husband was told that he must, of course, feel free to come and go as he wished.

Something had gone wrong with the hotel water heater and he had not been able to have a bath there.

I told him I would arrange for him to have one at the Palace.

It was during this performance that Princess Elizabeth walked into my rooms. She had come to ask me if I knew where the dogs' leashes were. But as soon as she came through my sitting-room door, she heard sounds of splashing from the bathroom.

George is not an unusually noisy bather. But men do tend to be more exuberant in the bath than women, and it was doubtless the first time Princess Elizabeth had heard the sounds which were now issuing forth.

"Good heavens, Crawfie," she said, smiling all over her face and round her eyes. "Whatever is that?" She must have thought I had brought a sea lion home.

I told her it was George taking a bath.

"Oh," she said, "your husband is having a bath and mine is taking the dogs round the garden for a walk."

Never a gameswoman myself, I fail to understand the joy that some women find in waving hockey sticks in the air and running about fields shouting to one another.

The Princesses would always get plenty of exercise from our walks, or riding, or cycling. They did not lack fresh air.

One day, while we were at the Royal Lodge, soon after King George had come to the Throne, I took them for a walk through the woods. They loved the woods and went there often. They were always interested in the varieties of wild flowers and the calls of the birds.

We were puzzled by the relics we found. No matter how peaceful or how secluded a wood is, you will always find somewhere in it a very old and rusty tin bath. We would often come upon these domestic relics —and others—quite a mile from the nearest road. The Princesses were very puzzled by them.

"But who would cart a bath all this way?" Princess Elizabeth asked me one day. "Why hide it in the middle of a wood?"

As the Princesses and I came back toward the tennis court which at the Royal Lodge is entirely surrounded by a cypress hedge so that only the nets can be seen from the house, we heard the sound of a ball being hit about the court.

Always curious, Princess Margaret pushed her head between two branches and peered through. "It's Mummy and Papa," she told me excitedly, "playing tennis."

After that we all had to see. The gate was on the far side of the court, quite a long way round. The hedge was not too firm so we clambered through.

The King and the Queen were playing alone. I thought what a pretty picture she made. She had on a cool print dress and a large shady hat, which, as usual, did not seem to disturb her at all.

Never having seen the Queen playing tennis before, I was amazed at the strength and accuracy of her backhand drive. The King was clearly not hitting his hardest. He was dressed in gray flannels and a light sport shirt open at the neck. I remember thinking how young and fit he looked.

The little girls were very excited and bounded about collecting the balls which the Queen hit with such force and obvious enjoyment.

The King was a very fine tennis player who had competed at Wimbledon, and it occurred to me that he might like the Princesses properly coached in the game.

Almost at the moment the thought entered my head, the King turned to the Queen and said to her: "Darling, Lilibet and Margaret must learn to play tennis, otherwise they won't be able to enjoy house parties when they grow up."

But something more pressing must have come up, for nothing more of tennis was heard for some years.

It was in the summer of 1944 that the subject was next mentioned. We were at Windsor Castle then, and saw the King and Queen only at week ends when they could be spared from the momentous tasks which were theirs.

One Monday, after the King and Queen had returned to London, Princess Elizabeth came to me in great excitement. "Papa thinks it's time we were taught tennis," she said. "He's getting a man to coach us."

I thought this a splendid idea. The court at Windsor lies below the level of the drive and is pleasantly situated in a sort of grass-covered hollow.

In King George V's time it was available to anyone

living in the Castle grounds; but few people had been using it lately. I visualized myself taking a book and deck chair and perhaps a bag of cherries and spending a pleasant time being critical.

But the Princesses had other ideas.

The tennis coach lived in Reading and made a journey every day to coach the Eton boys. He was a tall, athletic man of about forty with a pleasant, easy manner. On the first afternoon he arrived very early carrying a little bag.

A footman showed him a room where he could change. Presently he emerged in gleaming white flannels creased to razor sharpness.

Both the Princesses wore white. Princess Elizabeth looked particularly lovely, for she has long, slim legs which showed up well in her tennis costume.

The court lies off the main gravel drive and is approached through a small archway in the hedge which surrounds it. At the far end on the grass bank beyond the hollow in which it lies stands a small pavilion. I took up my post there and settled down to enjoy myself.

At first the coach showed the girls the rhythm of the strokes. He made them practice long sweeps with their rackets, rather as a swimming instructor puts his pupils through dry-land exercises.

These they did very prettily and competently. Then the coach went to the far end of the court and began lobbing balls over the net toward them.

It was now that my plans for a peaceful afternoon were shattered. Princess Elizabeth had a naturally powerful stroke, but as yet her aim was not so good as her intention. And Princess Margaret would as often as not hit the ball in the opposite direction from the one she intended.

I was quickly roused out of my comfortable chair to become ball boy. I certainly got plenty of exercise in that capacity!

Needless to say if anything was going on out of doors, the dogs could not be left out of it. So the Princesses would come down to the courts complete with the Corgis—three of them and a lion dog.

Immediately the whole game began to be enjoyed madly by the dogs, who tore about the court barking and running away with the balls.

In the ensuing chaos it became a wearing tussle for one to get a succession of balls out of "Cracker's" mouth, and eventually I put the leashes on the dogs, anchored the leashes to the legs of a basket chair on which I sat, and hoped for the best. The game continued to a series of agitated barks.

In all, the coach came about six times. At first the Princesses enjoyed it thoroughly. And they are always polite to strangers. If this man wanted them to make certain movements with their rackets, they would do their very best to oblige him.

As usual Princess Margaret was tired of it before Princess Elizabeth, who showed a natural eye. But

both were loth to run for the ball when it passed anywhere outside easy reach.

The coach was quick to realize this, and perhaps too
ready to give in to it. Perhaps he was shy. At any rate
he lobbed the balls back so that neither of them had
far to move to return them. But I was amused by his
private report to me when the lessons finished.

"Princess Elizabeth," he told me with great solemnity,
"has a very good natural eye for the game. But I am
afraid she'll never succeed at it until she forces herself
to run after the ball a bit more."

He was taking it very seriously.

But more important things were coming up for Princess Elizabeth. She was presently to join the Army,
and tennis, for the time being, was forgotten.

Part Five

THOSE who saw the Trooping of the Colors last summer will never forget the sight of Princess Elizabeth taking her place in the procession, serenely seated on her horse. As she rode to take the salute at the Trooping Ceremony, as a Colonel of the Grenadier Guards, she wore a scarlet and gold tunic and a black bearskin tricorne with a white plume, an exact copy of the hat worn by a Grenadier Colonel in 1754.

I have often felt that Queen Elizabeth was at her best on horseback. She sat there with a dignity it is difficult to describe: it was almost as if she was molded into position.

Normally, of course, she rode astride. But for the dignified parade, in which she made her first appearance in 1948, she felt that sidesaddle would be more appropriate.

It was arranged that she should take part in the parade some months before while she was still on the South African tour. She did not then possess a side-saddle, which is a beautifully made piece of leather specially fitted for the individual rider. Accordingly, orders were sent home to have one prepared for her, and this she found waiting her on her return.

With that thoroughness which is so typical of her she then set about practicing with it, so that when the parade came she would be, so to speak, saddle-perfect.

As everyone knows, she carried her part off magnificently. But on that occasion her father was there to see her through. This year he was ill and could not be so close.

But again she played her part with all that skill we have come to expect as Queen Elizabeth's way. She sat her horse with a grace which brought murmurs of admiration from the huge crowd who came to watch.

"It makes me think," one courtier told me, "of that well-known picture of Queen Elizabeth reviewing her troops from horseback before the Armada."

Many people made similar comments. But for Princess Elizabeth the main interest in the procession must have been her feeling that here at last was some concrete help she could give her beloved father.

I have often commented on the strong sense of duty which animates her. Although the strain is obviously great, Queen Elizabeth has taken on her tasks with equanimity. For these are the functions to which her life has been dedicated. This is the goal toward which all those long walks and quiet, confidential chats with her father through the years had been directed.

Now is beginning to appear the end of which Winston Churchill was thinking when he spared so much of his valuable time during the war to chat with her of world affairs.

If I were writing a novel I could have as well called this portion "A true story—A Bird in a Gilded Cage," or "The Prisoner in the Palace."

Every so often a Member of Parliament rises to inquire how the Royal Grants and Allowances are being spent, sometimes implying that the money might be better directed on some other path.

But those who have read *Mother and Queen* will know how simple a life the Royal Family lead. Nothing is wasted. Every piece of material, ball of string, sheet of paper is put away to be saved for the next time. Whole rooms in Buckingham Palace are filled with crates containing things left over from three reigns.

What money the Royal Family draw is intended to help them keep up their position, growing more expensive every year, and entertain in the lavish way which is expected of them.

Few people comprehend the rigorous routine their position thrusts upon the Royal Family. Imagine every moment of your day mapped out sometimes months ahead, not only for today and tomorrow, but almost for this time next year.

To the Royal Family, committed to open a bazaar here, attend a dinner there, lay a stone somewhere else, there are no idle moments. Seldom can they suddenly decide to go to bed early with a book, or take a week end in the country—the privilege of so many of their subjects. Too many people depend on their presence to allow them to indulge whims.

Regardless of mood or health—short of actual illness, and the Royal tradition there is Spartan—their job is to appear and be the center of all eyes.

On Princess Elizabeth's desk in her study at Clarence House there stood a large, square, leather-bound calendar embossed with her initial *E* in gold on one of the facings.

It was divided into three divisions—morning, afternoon, and evening—and each division contained those functions she was committed to attend.

As I have told, her secretary would come in with the pile of letters she receives asking her to appear all over the country.

Those she decided to attend were entered on the calendar at once and the secretary made a copy in his own diary.

Gradually the spaces filled up until I have seen six or seven appointments for one day—a round which imposed a great strain on the Princess.

Besides the physical effort needed to complete such

a program, which comes up not once or twice but every day of her life, there is the greater one of never having a moment to relax and be herself.

Always the spotlight of public interest follows her, exploring her most private and personal moments in a way which few of her subjects would stand.

It is right, with the Constitution formed as it is, that Royal Grants should be discussed by the Parliament which passes them. But it cannot be pleasant to have your income, needs, and expenses attacked by the House of Commons and the result of their debate published all over the world.

I well remember the embarrassed air which hung over Buckingham Palace while the allowances paid yearly to Princess Elizabeth and Prince Philip were being debated.

From the age of eleven the Princess received a yearly income of £6,000—granted her out of the King's Civil List of £410,000.

At twenty-one this income was raised to £15,000 annually, and at the time of her marriage to £30,000 with extra grants for the upkeep of Clarence House.

To those who think these figures large I would point out what inflated expenses Royalty have to bear. Princess Elizabeth had to furnish her house literally "fit for a king" to live in.

It would not have been in the country's interests for the Heiress Presumptive to live in a suburban bungalow.

Just as, when she went abroad, the Princess was our Number One Ambassadress, so, at home, hers was the home which typified the country.

To maintain it she had to employ a staff far larger than her private tastes dictated. She had to have a Comptroller to handle the complex problems of her household and manage her finances; a secretary to handle the huge mail which came to her daily and deal with her appointments and those callers who needed her assistance; there were the kitchen, the backstairs staff needed to support the house in the style which Parliament felt would make it a credit to the country, and there were pensioners grown old in Royal service who had to be provided for in their retirement.

All these expenses drain away at what may seem an unnecessarily large figure.

On top of them was the major outlay of entertaining foreign dignitaries who visit the country and cannot be entertained by a sandwich and a cup of tea. They must be met with the pomp and ceremony suitable to their rank.

Banquets and garden parties sometimes cost the King as much as £3,000 each. All this had to come out of his grant. And, similarly, the Princess's smaller-scale entertaining came out of hers.

This they accepted as part of their duty. But it could not be pleasant for them to have to face, on the top of that burden, criticism of the monies they are allowed, so very little of which remains for their private amusement.

No girl in love and yet not publicly joined by engagement to the man she loves welcomes prying into her private feelings.

Yet that is what Princess Elizabeth had to put up with all through that long, trying time before she and Prince Philip could face the world as future man and wife.

Although that sense of duty I have stressed so often in these pages is one which made her destiny of the highest importance in the Queen's life, do not think that this curiosity did not cost her dear.

I saw her shaken by the sometimes coarse but no doubt kindly-meant interest in her affairs taken by some of the public she saw on her day's duty.

I felt the strain she was under, watched the way her eyes would sometimes stray to Prince Philip, knowing that in her heart she must be saying, "Why can't I marry the man I love? Why must there be this pitiless delay?"

It does not require great depths of imagination to visualize the struggle which must have taken place inside her; the desire of every girl in love to be with the man she loves, conditioned by her training which taught her that Royalty are not as other people—not in any superior way, but only in the disciplined position imposed on them.

How often she must have longed to throw it all up, to leave the court which turned her private life into a public discussion and run away.

And yet she did not do that, however great the temptation must have been.

I am reminded of what someone very near to the King told me about his feelings at the time of the Abdication.

King Edward VIII had forfeited his crown and thrown the country into a turmoil. Such a thing had not happened to Great Britain for hundreds of years, and it is true to say that there was no precedent to guide the Government's actions.

It was assumed that the next eldest son would automatically inherit the Throne. But some in high places questioned this. It was thought that Abdication was such a serious step it changed the course of normal things.

"Why thrust this Crown and its great responsibilities on a man whose every action through life has shown his dislike of publicity and love of the quiet life?" they said. "The Duke of York has no sons; he suffers a speech defect which make every public appearance an agony to him. Let us take the chance this whirlpool in our midst has given us to appoint the Duke of Kent King. He already has a son; he is a man whose temperament equips him more easily to take the center place in life. Spare the Duke of York a task which he must consider a burden."

But the King had too strong a sense of the duty he owed the country to take this easy way out. I remember the pain in his eyes, the pallor this new responsibility cast over his features, which seemed suddenly to age.

But his main concern, my friend told me, was not for the weight the Crown would place upon his shoulders, but the thought of the weight one day to be transferred to the shoulders of his elder daughter.

He was loth to condemn her to a lifetime of public servitude, where she would have no peace and never be allowed the quiet domestic enjoyment which is every woman's birthright.

In spite of the many restrictions put on the personal liberty of Royalty, such as their being unable to choose flat-heeled shoes for public appearances, or hats that would hide their faces, the last century has brought to them small freedoms denied to their grandparents.

One of these is the carrying about of handbags and money. The days when a lady-in-waiting used to pay for any small thing that took the Royal fancy is over; both Princess Elizabeth and Princess Margaret carried bags and two or three pounds in ready cash like any ordinary girl or woman. They cashed their own checks through their Comptroller, put the notes into neat notecases made to match their handbags, and loose silver into little purses.

From this money they paid direct in the shops for things they wished to buy. Most of their shopping excursions took place in Aberdeen when they were staying at Balmoral.

It is not generally known, I think, that Royalty pay for everything they have. The King was insistent that all goods supplied to the Palace be paid for, and although tradespeople would be pleased to supply the Royal Household free in order to have the honor of serving them, this was something the King would not accept, although he was, in fact, the poorest monarch since William IV.

The Royal Family also pay railway fares. The only time they do not pay to travel is when they are on a battleship or using a Viking of the King's Flight.

The matter of so little personal liberty—taken for granted by all of us—is something that I have thought must be very hard to bear if you are a woman.

Never for Princess Elizabeth the happy prowlings round the stores comparing the prices, colors, and textures of the materials for a new coat or dress; not for her the quest to get calf or suède shoes to match *exactly* the color of her handbag, and the excitement that lasts through several days when the tricky piece of shopping is satisfactorily accomplished.

All that personal, exciting, challenging side of choosing a wardrobe was taken out of her hands by her dressmaker, shoemaker, and milliner.

The exact color of the main garment is given to the tradesmen and then the accessories arrive, perfect, beautiful, costly, without the personal effort which makes shopping so large a part of the whole intriguing adventure of a woman's life.

I do not say that Queen Elizabeth does not choose her own clothes. Of course she does, but within circumscribed limits. She has to remember, for instance, that however much she might long to wear a certain color, she cannot do so if it is a shade that will tone in with and get lost among a large crowd and so make it difficult for her to be easily and immediately seen by the loyal crowds who congregate wherever she is to make a public appearance, in the hope of catching a glimpse of her.

There might be times, too, when in the interest of trade she is asked to wear a certain material, a certain style of shoe to give it that boost that will make the whole world buy it.

However much that particular thing may be anathema to her she will do it if she knows that, by sponsoring it, work and prosperity may be guaranteed to millions of her subjects all over the world.

All the year round there is someone, somewhere, who has something that would be helped by Royal patronage. Lengths of tweed, wool, silk, rayon, cotton of new design and texture, millions of lengths, are considered every day as an offering to her, for it is known that her acceptance will create a boom in the particular product.

But all that is offered is not accepted. The Queen wants to know all the details of anything that she is offered: who made it, and why, and if her acceptance is

· *153*

likely on the one hand to show undue favoritism, or, on the other, to inspire productivity that will materially help this country and the Empire.

When she knows all these details she makes a decision, and whoever it was who offered it to her in the first place gets a charming personal note from her.

In the case of textiles that are accepted, these are not always immediately made up into suits or coats. They are ticketed and stored against the day when she may need them.

But what a temptation it must be if a particularly beautiful length of tweed is offered to her, of which she would like to have a suit, to have to forego it because to have it made up would necessitate a completely new range of accessories, and that is an extravagance upon which she must not embark.

After all, she must set an example, and since early childhood both Princesses were taught by their mother and grandmother that nothing must be wasted.

You and I have a choice in the matter. If it suits us to sell for a mere song the good brown handbag we bought last winter and the shoes that go with it because we've seen a much nicer outfit in blue and want entirely new accessories, we're at liberty to do as we like about it, and no one any the wiser.

And perhaps, every now and again, a piece of seemingly wild extragance is the birthright of every woman if she enjoys it and feels better and smarter for having thrown her old shoes and bag over the wind-mill.

But not for the Queen. The particularly heady pleasure, which is never understood by men, but always by other women, will always be denied to her.

So, too, are other such temperamental escapes and outbursts. The wilful pleasure of using the whole of one week's egg rations the first week that eggs become less scarce on a mouth-watering cake, and spending the whole of Saturday afternoon singing away in the kitchen as it bakes, is a feminine delight so natural, so normal, that few of us stop for a moment to think about the privacy and the liberty in our own homes, and rejoice that we were not born to a rank that denies its holder so simple a womanly pleasure as this.

As against the more simple pleasures which just do not occur in the life of a Queen, there are, you may think, tremendous compensations. Such as her beautiful jewels which seem to sparkle even more brightly against the warmth and texture of her lovely skin.

Imagine having jewel cases full of the most exquisite diamonds, rubies, emeralds, and pearls, so that there is something to suit every dress, every occasion, you might think!

But think again. Can there be so much pleasure in having so many? Isn't there infinitely more joy in the small, intimate, semi-precious stone, chosen with tremendous care especially for you to match your eyes, to enhance your skin, rather than a load of Crown jewels which you might not care for?

Some women dislike emeralds, others say sapphires do not suit them, and there are women who will never wear diamonds at all, saying they are too hard. In this again the Queen has no personal choice. If a public occasion warrants the sparkle of diamonds, on they must go whether she likes them or not, and often a matching tiara which is a heavy, cumbrous, tiresome thing for a young girl to have to wear throughout an evening.

She has one tiara which she especially loves. It is an exquisite thing made of diamonds in the form of delicate marguerites. It can be taken apart and worn as a necklace, two clips, and a bracelet, and when she unpacked it she was delighted. Later, showing it to me, she exclaimed, with eyes as bright as the diamonds she was holding: "Isn't it a lovely thing, Crawfie?"

Although so much of the life Queen Elizabeth has to lead must be a burden to her, there is one side of her public life I know will always grip and enthuse her.

From her earliest moments she has always had that interest in soldiers, uniforms, and military customs which so animated her father.

I remember on one of the earliest of the Monday afternoon excursions on which Queen Mary used to take us, watching the little Princess as we walked slowly round an exhibition of tapestries.

Queen Mary is very knowledgeable about such things.

Queen Elizabeth is presented with an Indian suit for Prince Charles on her Canadian tour.

Queen Elizabeth and Prince Philip leaving church in Ste. Agathe des Monts, Quebec.

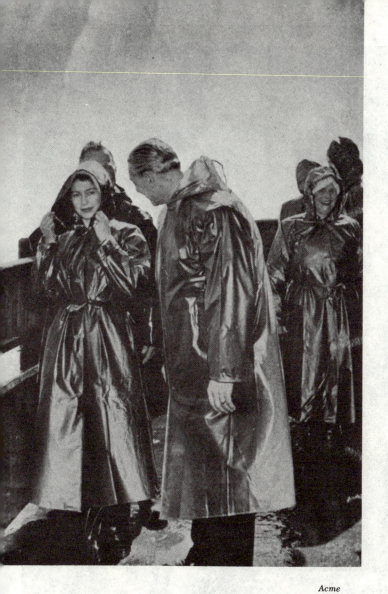

The Queen saw everything, even Niagara Falls from below.

Queen Elizabeth in cowgirl costume enjoys a
square dance in Ottawa.

The Queen and Prince Philip with their special guard of Canadian Mounties.

In Washington Margaret Truman takes
the Royal visitors sightseeing.

The Queen inspects the Declaration of Independence and the Constitution.

The Royal Couple pay tribute at the Tomb of the Unknown Soldier.

Queen Elizabeth and Prince Philip leave the tomb of George
Washington, where they had just placed a wreath.

Queen Elizabeth and her husband walk down the
steps of the House of Representatives as U. S.
Marines stand guard.

The Queen and Prince Philip admire Walter Beach's twenty-six Boy Scout merit badges.

Acme

Queen Elizabeth chats with President Truman at the formal dinner given for her by the Trumans.

Queen Elizabeth at a garden party, Nairobi, Kenya Colony, February 1, 1952.

The Queen visits the Pumwani African Maternity Home in Nairobi, only a few days before she received news of her father's death.

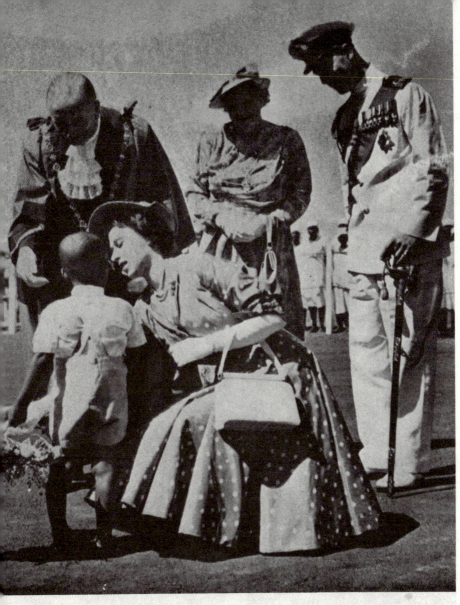

Queen Elizabeth helps out the bashful
three-year-old Prince Salim.

Elizabeth II is proclaimed Queen at Windsor beneath the statue of her great-great-grandmother, Queen Victoria, on February 8, 1952.

"Now take this one," she would say, and then tell us something fascinating about the way in which it had been made and where it had hung in the past. She has a fund of knowledge about such matters which is almost awe-inspiring.

But though usually Princess Elizabeth used to hang on to every word her grandmother uttered, on this occasion I noticed her attention straying.

I followed her eyes and saw, across the room, three tall Guardsmen in their khaki uniforms. Princess Elizabeth was watching them intently, with that fascinated concentration a more modern child might bestow on a visiting film star. She never took her eyes off them during the whole tour we made of the exhibition.

I was amused when we got her home to 145 Piccadilly to notice that her first thought was to tell Mummy of this wonderful experience.

Her mother was always very gentle with the children. She would take a great interest in their day's doings, and greet them with a "Well, darlings, and what have you seen today?"

This time Princess Elizabeth wasted no time on repeating the lore about the tapestry which Queen Mary had passed on to us. Instead, she ran to her mother and hugged her, saying, "Oh, Mummy, Mummy. There were three *soldiers* there!"

That interest in things military has remained with her. She would always stand fascinated at the window of 145 while the Guard marched across Hyde Park Corner in the mornings, splendid in their scarlet uniforms.

"Oh, look, Crawfie," she would say excitedly. "Aren't they pretty?"

I used sometimes to see the same expression of interest cross her face while she watched a parade of soldiers at a much later date.

However much the routine of her life may weigh on her, I am sure the military side of it will never bore her.

One of Queen Elizabeth's most charming traits was exhibited in her insistence that her sister, Princess Margaret, should be given all the attention due her. This has persisted from childhood.

When Princess Elizabeth, even as a very small girl, felt that visitors or friends were making so much fuss of her that Princess Margaret was in danger of being neglected, Princess Elizabeth would seize the first opportunity to say, "And now you must come and see my little sister."

The first time I saw that thoughtful gesture was when Princess Margaret was so young that she was still using her perambulator, but old enough to enjoy having people round her and to resent finding herself alone when she awoke from the afternoon nap. Princess Elizabeth made it her business to see that her sister was soon a center of admiration.

This trait is still with her. Since her marriage it has

had less opportunity for expression; and besides, Princess Margaret, with a personality that draws interesting people to her, never has a chance to feel neglected.

And Queen Elizabeth has passed on to her own children this considerate habit. An old ghillie who had spent years in the Royal Service at Balmoral and had just retired was full of praise for Queen Elizabeth, whose charm and thoughtfulness had caused her to be reverenced by servants not only in her own home but wherever she went.

"And doesn't little Prince Charles take after his mother!" said the ghillie in broad Scots which has to be translated to be readable.

"Everybody loves him here in Scotland; the servants and tenants flock to see him. After a few moments of being the center of admiration the little boy always takes the hand of the nearest person to him—usually a woman—and leads her to where Princess Anne is sitting up perkily in her pram. 'And now,' he says, 'you must all come and see my little sister.'"

I can imagine some of the joy that Queen Elizabeth will have in her children when they are old enough to learn poetry by heart.

Of course Prince Charles already knows many of the old, familiar nursery rhymes that delight all children. But soon, I am sure, he will find a great deal of fun repeating A. A. Milne's happy little marching song: "They're Changing Guard at Buckingham Palace."

BUCKINGHAM PALACE *

They're changing guard at Buckingham Palace—
Christopher Robin went down with Alice.
Alice is marrying one of the guard.
"A soldier's life is terrible hard,"
Says Alice.

They're changing guard at Buckingham Palace—
Christopher Robin went down with Alice.
We saw a guard in a sentry-box.
"One of the sergeants looks after their socks,"
Says Alice.

They're changing guard at Buckingham Palace—
Christopher Robin went down with Alice.
We looked for the King, but he never came.
"Well, God take care of him, all the same,"
Says Alice.

They're changing guard at Buckingham Palace—
Christopher Robin went down with Alice.
They've great big parties inside the grounds.
"I wouldn't be King for a hundred pounds,"
Says Alice.

---

* Copyright, 1924, by E. P. Dutton & Co., Inc., from the book *When We Were Very Young*, by A. A. Milne.

> *They're changing guard at Buckingham Palace—*
> *Christopher Robin went down with Alice.*
> *A face looked out, but it wasn't the King's.*
> *"He's much too busy a-signing things,"*
>
> > *Says Alice.*

> *They're changing guard at Buckingham Palace—*
> *Christopher Robin went down with Alice.*
> *"Do you think the King knows all about me?"*
> *"Sure to, dear, but it's time for tea,"*
>
> > *Says Alice.*

It was Queen Elizabeth's favorite poem when she was a child. One of the lesson periods I most enjoyed during the time I taught the Princesses was that which we devoted to poetry. My own interest in the music of words is deep. I get great pleasure from their formation and the rhythms and rhymes they make.

I tried to pass on that love to the Princesses. In Princess Margaret's case I was instantly successful; she has a very strong sense of the value of words and loves to use them colorfully.

Queen Elizabeth, too, enjoys poetry. But hers is a more conservative taste than mine. I like to read what is called modern verse. I like seeing new patterns of words and experimenting with the melodies they form. But I was never able to imbue her with this enthusiasm.

"Oh, do stop!" she would say while I was reading from the works of some modern poet. "I don't understand a word of it. What *is* the man trying to say?"

She loves the more rhythmical jingling works of Kipling, Tennyson, and Longfellow. *Hiawatha* was one of her favorite pieces, and "They're Changing Guard at Buckingham Palace" she knew by heart. Before we left 145 Piccadilly she would act the whole piece through, taking each character in turn.

She particularly enjoyed playing the sentry, stamping out the somewhat clockwork movements with great dignity. Sometimes I was press-ganged into playing the other sentry, whom, in the course of the poem, she met in the middle of the playroom floor and turned away from with all the enthusiastic stamping and crashing of feet which accompany an actual changing of the Guard.

When we moved to Buckingham Palace, the old interest was quickened. We would go out and watch the sentries, to be enthralled by their rigid efficiency. "Aren't they handsome, Crawfie?" Princess Elizabeth would say admiringly. She likes a smart, well-cut uniform, and the Guards are always impressive.

I can see the eyes of Prince Charles and Princess Anne shine as brightly as their mother's at the sight of the soldiers marching and wheeling, sometimes with the sun shining from their bright buttons, sometimes with the rain shining on their polished leather.

And I can see the children marching up and down in their playroom of Clarence House, enjoying the game in happy ignorance of the fact that one day the sentries outside would be "Soldiers of the Queen" to their mother.

Part Six

LITTLE did anyone realize, watching the two children playing, how soon those Guardsmen were to become "Soldiers of the Queen"—and in what strange and tragic circumstances.

Princess Elizabeth's hour of destiny was approaching fast when anxiety for the health of the King reached its height in the autumn of 1951 on the news of his impending grave operation, and the postponement of her visit to Canada.

How well I remember those dark September days of 1951 when George, my husband, and I, like all His Majesty's subjects at home and overseas, centered our thoughts and prayers for the health of the beloved patient in Buckingham Palace.

Never had the Royal Family seemed so near and

dear as when they gathered at the Palace on that critical week end of his operation. Princess Elizabeth stayed there for seven anxious hours with her mother and Princess Margaret, while Queen Mary, the Duke of Gloucester, and the Princess Royal waited at Marlborough House.

Only the Family themselves will ever know the effort it cost them to hide their private anxiety behind the quiet faith and trust in God that showed on their faces.

The leaden weight of those days fell especially on the shoulders of Princess Elizabeth. Her departure on what was to have been a "second" honeymoon in Canada had been summarily postponed, with thoughts of the continuity of the Monarchy inevitably in mind.

Before the burden of vigil for her father could be lifted from her shoulders, another burden, the duties of Empire, had to be added. As soon as the King's immediate danger had diminished, the Princess had to leave for Montreal with Prince Philip, her first major tour without the King and Queen.

I think the whole Western world must have applauded her courage, as responsibilities of intimidating volume accumulated on every side.

A few hours before the Royal airplane's departure, plans were made for her fateful visit to East Africa, Australia, and New Zealand, in place of her father. I can imagine what she would say, as she has said to me: "I've just got to do it. It's my job."

The Story of Britain's New Sovereign

In Canada, on the most strenuous Royal tour ever undertaken, there were often tears in her eyes when the conversation turned to her father's illness, or even at banquets when the ritualistic toast was given to "The King!" She sought to reassure herself constantly by transatlantic telephone calls asking about his recovery.

The tension she clearly suffered did nothing to impair her graciousness, but the essential warmth of her personality tended to be overshadowed by the strain of the hectic routine of inspecting Guards of Honor, visits to City Halls, the presentation of City Councillors, receiving bouquets, and addresses of welcome. The Duke of Edinburgh spread the cloak of his smiling protection around her, in a foretaste of one of his many future roles.

One day she seemed particularly tense as she sat stiff and erect in a limousine, ready to depart for yet another official function. The Duke entered the car and began a lively conversation with her. She received from him a gift which every wife realizes is priceless, a compliment on how attractive she looked in the dress she was wearing. She relaxed, with a smile that the crowds shared with her husband.

Queen Elizabeth's sense of duty drives her to the limits of her strength and endurance today. She governed her onerous tours by two broad principles, while the actual day-to-day details, of course, were worked out by the country whose guest she was.

She insists that she be seen by as many people as humanly possible, and she asks to see as much of the country as she can, whether by car, train, airplane, or ship.

She stipulates, too, something that comes straight from her heart—that special consideration be given to the children and the ex-service men and women on all occasions.

As the days passed on her Canadian tour, the continuingly favorable reports of the King's doctors and the Duke of Edinburgh's infectious high spirits transformed the Princess. Canadians caught sight of the happy, graceful girl I used to watch in the Palace ballrooms when, at Government House in Ottawa, she danced lightheartedly in flared blue skirt and brown checked blouse.

Since her childhood she has heard the Scottish reels that the band played there, but the "hoe down" was completely new to her. After one brief lesson, she acquitted herself handsomely to the music of such Western favorites as "Rock Valley" and "The Farmer's Jamboree."

As I have said, Queen Elizabeth, like all of us, lives and learns, but she learns faster than most—as she is showing us already in her young reign.

If Canada were already in love with her, that love deepened as the crowds noticed the little, human details of her appearance: easing her feet out of fashionable, high-heeled pumps; her hatless, hair-blown ride beside her husband in a racing open car; her hairdressing appointment soon afterward, where the sympathetic woman hairdresser reported later that "she was homesick for her children."

She telephoned Clarence House to talk to Prince Charles from Eaglecrest, the ski lodge retreat in the Laurentian Mountains, set in a landscape straight from an old-fashioned Christmas card.

Before a roaring log fire she painstakingly wrote the thank-you notes, which she never forgets, and outside the lodge she was almost a girl again, freed of public servitude for a romp over the snow, while the Duke of Edinburgh built a snowman and threw snowballs at her.

But such moments would be few. She knew that then. She knew it earlier, when on her twenty-first birthday she said—in words that still move me as I think of them: "I declare before you all that my whole life, whether it be short or long, shall be devoted to your service and the service of our great Imperial family to which we all belong.

"But I shall not have the strength to carry out that resolution alone unless you join in it with me, as I now invite you to do."

With the ladies-in-waiting, a valet, footman, and a casket full of jewels, Princess Elizabeth and the Duke of Edinburgh visited the capital of the United States for what one newspaper account accurately described as "the best party Washington ever had." As any one of us would, she had saved a new velvet hat for her journey south of the Canadian border.

I have always found the people of North America generous and demonstrative to a point where such retiring souls as I am almost overwhelmed. I think Princess Elizabeth may have experienced a similar feeling during the nearly 20,000 miles of her journeying in that awe-inspiring continent.

She was apt to be so beset by affectionate crowds that she would find herself separated even from her husband. And Washington had seldom seen such numbers on its broad avenues as when the Royal party arrived.

President Truman himself declared: "Never before have we had such a wonderful young couple that so completely captured the hearts of all of us."

His beaming smile showed that, so far as he was concerned, he regarded the British Princess almost as "one of the family"—which, on the feminine side, wore new dresses for this celebration. That feminine side of his family, Mrs. Truman and his daughter Margaret, shared his opinions.

From the President's first "I thank you, dear," spoken in answer to the formal arrival speech, to his farewell urging that the Royal couple should visit him again and "bring the children," those forty-five packed hours in the United States afforded our future Queen a new vista of the world in which she now plays a vital part as ruler of its most powerful monarchy.

Earlier in the book I wrote of her dislike of the sea. Her departure from North America in a tossing ferry-boat illustrates how her stern self-discipline has overcome that antipathy. It was the wildest and most dramatic hour of the entire tour.

A nor'wester was sending sixteen-foot waves dashing against the wharf of the rocky, storm-beaten fishing village of Portugal Cove in Newfoundland, Britain's oldest North American colony.

The sturdy villagers, in clean blue denims and salt-caked boots, stood drenched by cold rain and spray, waiting a weary while until all the baggage and presents were loaded aboard the ferry, *Maneco*. The last of the full ton of gifts pressed on the Royal visitors during their stay arrived on the spot, in the shape of fresh cod, just caught in the Newfoundland fishing grounds.

Then the Princess went aboard, in open-toed shoes and with a beige rain wrap over her mink coat, to receive the final good wishes on the pitching deck, while the Duke stood by her on steady sailor's legs. The fisherfolk were singing "The Squid-Jiggin' Ground" and other folksongs.

"Holy smoke, what a bustle, all hands are excited," the words run. "It's a wonder to me nobody is drowned." A somber lyric to hear when you face a rough trip in a tiny boat over furious water! The Princess concentrated not on herself but on others, as always.

As the ferry scraped alongside the waiting *Empress of Scotland,* which was to carry her back to England, she noticed one of the crew of the liner with his head through a porthole watching the little ship's approach.

She instantly saw the danger, and before anyone else had noticed it she cried, "Mind your head! Mind your head! Look out!"

Then the "sea-king's daughter from over the sea" as the poet Tennyson described another Princess, said *au revoir* to Canada aboard the *Empress.* Fresh and excited, she suggested, in an instinctive thought to put everyone at their ease, "Let's have lunch right away!" This, after a bumpy sea trip in wild weather, from someone who dislikes the sea!

A British Princess can never expect too much from the weather. Torrential rain fell from the November clouds when the Royal train arrived in London from the Liverpool docks where the *Empress* had tied up.

Those who watched saw an unforgettable tableau as the train pulled in. Prince Charles, hatless and with his golden hair brushed until it shone, jumped up and down with excitement as he sighted his parents.

Those thoughtless few who sometimes criticized Princess Elizabeth for her absences from her children must surely have sensed how painful those separations were if they had seen her then.

On the platform she almost knelt down on the red carpet to hug her son close. Father-like, the Duke ruffled the little boy's hair. "How he seems to have grown!" he said, while Prince Charles, as excited children will, wiped his hand across his cheeks.

The Queen and Princess Margaret were there on the platform; the King, of course, with Queen Mary and Princess Anne, waited in the Palace. Then the waiting thousands in the great area outside were rewarded for their endurance in the rain by the sight of the little, dearly-loved Family group standing reunited on the balcony in the twilight of an autumn day.

Princess Elizabeth spent her first quiet evening in six weeks at home in the peace of Clarence House, a few sweet hours of personal liberty that marked the end of one tour with another following on its heels.

And so we come to that fateful last day of January, 1952, when the King stood at London Airport waving his daughter good-by as she and the Duke of Edinburgh set off on their flight to Africa and the Commonwealth tour they were undertaking in his place.

For forty minutes the King stood bareheaded in a biting, wintry wind, and after he had waved what was to be his last good-by to his daughter, he followed her plane with his eyes until it was no more than a faint speck in a gray sky.

Who knows what feelings were in his heart when at last he turned away—and what were the feelings in the heart of his daughter as she sped across the world on her Royal mission?

Twice within six months Princess Elizabeth had been called upon to endure parting from her father after a grievous operation, for which the nation's prayers were asked, when all her instincts as a daughter must have cried out to stay by his side.

All over the world newspapers carried stories of the progress of the *Atalanta,* Princess Elizabeth's airplane, and her safe arrival in Africa, where she was met by four hundred African chiefs resplendent in plumed headdresses and leopard skins.

The hearts of millions of ordinary men and women going about their humdrum tasks were daily warmed by the happy, carefree pictures of the Royal couple in their informal moments in the first few days of their great tour.

Pictures of the Princess with her camera eagerly "shooting" lion, stalking through the jungle while a nearby guard moved with his rifle at the alert; pictures of her and the Duke of Edinburgh in the Royal Lodge —the wedding gift of the people of Kenya—joyous, unworried pictures we all loved to see; pictures, like those of any young married couple, of the Princess and her husband enjoying the peace and beauty of their home.

But the sands of time were ebbing fast . . .

In Britain, King George was at his beloved Sandringham, scene of his birth, living a country life. The Queen and Princess Margaret were with him. Daily he enjoyed one of his favorite sports, shooting, with a few chosen friends from among his neighbors.

The fifth of February was a particularly lovely crisp winter's day in Norfolk, and the King enjoyed one of his best day's sport. That evening he made arrangements for the next day, and before she said good night to him Princess Margaret suggested that he might like to make an early start in the morning.

The King went to bed and his valet brought him his usual nightcap, a cup of hot chocolate. The King wished him good night in a cheerful voice and settled to read a book.

Across the world, Princess Elizabeth and the Duke of Edinburgh were spending the night in the picturesque "Treetops," a four-room hotel some distance from their Royal Lodge, which is built in a giant fig tree overlooking a water hole so that its visitors may observe animals by night.

The Princess arrived wearing a bush shirt and brown slacks, and was afforded a magnificent spectacle of the big game of Kenya. When she arrived at the beginning of the forest trail she heard that no less than forty elephants were gathered around "Treetops."

And when she arrived at her "hotel" she was asked to climb the ladder slowly so as not to disturb one elephant who was by a pool only ten yards away. Thirty-five elephants and eleven calves appeared while the Royal party were having tea, and after dusk eight rhinos were spotted.

It was around midnight when the Princess retired.

After breakfast next day she delayed her return to the Royal Lodge for an hour, enjoying the first sunlit moments of the African morning, amusedly watching the antics of a family of baboons which had climbed to the "Treetops" windows and were grabbing slices of sweet potato laid on the sills. Then she and the Duke set off for the Royal Lodge, unaware of the terrible news which awaited them.

On that morning of February 6th there was silence in the King's bedroom at Sandringham. His valet, entering with his usual cup of tea, could not rouse him. Beside his bed, its bookmarker set, lay the book the King had been reading when he fell asleep some time before midnight.

At 10.45 A.M. the news of his death was announced.

And in one of his most moving broadcasts, Mr. Churchill revealed that the King had known that from day to day his life hung by a thread:

"The King walked with death as if death were a companion, an acquaintance whom he recognized and did not fear.

"In the end death came as a friend, and, after a happy day of sunshine and sport, after 'Good night' to those who had loved him best, he fell asleep as every man or woman who strives to fear God and nothing else may hope to do."

In Africa the first intimation was given to the Princess's staff by a local newspaper reporter. Lieutenant Colonel Martin Charteris, the Princess's private secretary, hardly crediting the news, sought confirmation from London.

It was the Duke of Edinburgh who gently told his unsuspecting wife the news of her father's death and that she was now Queen of England.

When she first understood what he was saying, she

wept, but, said Lieutenant Colonel Charteris, she took the news "bravely, like a Queen."

It was the first time in history that a British monarch had acceded to the Throne in Africa.

At once the new Queen gave orders to return, and through streets lined with rows of silent, sorrowing Africans she drove to her airplane. But—so typical of her—before she left she did not forget to give her personal thanks to every person, white or colored, who had attended her during her stay.

So began the *Atalanta's* 4,444-mile return flight, to Britain and the airport from which only six days previously the King had waved his daughter farewell. Tropical thunderstorms delayed the passage of the Royal plane, and escorting aircraft carried land and sea rescue gear throughout that sad journey from continent to continent upon which the attention of the whole world was fixed.

In Britain, the time-worn wheels of Royal and State procedure for the proclamation of a new monarch and a royal funeral were already turning with all their historic significance when the sad-faced young Queen alighted at London Airport, to be greeted by her uncle, the Duke of Gloucester, who handed her a sealed envelope from her bereaved mother; and her moist-eyed veteran Prime Minister, Mr. Churchill.

On the next day the Proclamation of Queen Elizabeth the Second, Head of the Commonwealth, took place in London and throughout the Commonwealth, with all its rich traditional ceremony.

Then the Queen drove to Sandringham to meet her mother and to take her last sight of the father who for twenty-five years she had so dearly loved.

Before she left London Queen Elizabeth made her accession Declaration and, in a clear, firm voice, the new Queen said:

"By the sudden death of my dear father I am called to assume the duties and responsibilities of sovereignty . . . the grief which his loss brings us is shared among us all.

"My heart is too full for me to say more to you to-day than that I shall always work, as my father did throughout his reign . . . to advance the happiness and prosperity of my peoples, spread as they are all the world over.

"I know that in my resolve to follow his shining example of service and devotion I shall be inspired by the loyalty and affection of those whose Queen I have been called upon to be.

"I pray that God will help me to discharge worthily the heavy task that has been laid upon me so early in my life."

When the Queen was a little child there was one diminutive name her father loved to call her by. And on the all-white wreath which lay on his coffin in the church at Sandringham, was the inscription:

"DARLING PAPA—FROM LILIBET"

Part Seven

QUEEN ELIZABETH was the first of her line to be proclaimed Head of the Commonwealth.

Millions of people of many races and colors are bound
not only to her but also to one another by their common allegiance. This allegiance is dependent on many
factors, including mutual assistance and defense; but
the one factor that gives meaning to all the rest is the
affection in which the Throne is held.

When the world was stunned by the shock of her
father's sudden death, Princess Elizabeth faced the
news—and all that lay before her—with the courage
with which she faces all crises.

For the Heir to the Throne private grief must be
swallowed up in the office and the task must be merged
in the continuity of the Monarchy.

It is her job in life to be in a sense "owned" by her people. No longer does the monarch command in the old absolute way; the sovereign is the personage who symbolizes for all of us the perfection we would most like to attain.

Queen Elizabeth has always been aware of this, at first dimly but now with crystal clearness.

Learned men outside the Empire, admiring the success of kingship as an imperial institution, have mastered the reasons and have written books which tell us more about our history than many of us knew ourselves.

Discussing monarchy, "It works!" they say, as if they had discovered something new, and they devote hundreds of pages to explaining how and why it works. On one thing all such commentators agree—the Commonwealth without a monarch is unthinkable.

It is comforting to remember that some of our greatest rulers, in the ages of our greatest glory—such as the Elizabethan age and the Victorian age—have been Queens.

Inspired by the gracious woman we now know as Queen Elizabeth, shall we see a second Elizabethan age, marked not only by the resurgence of the old spirit of adventure but also by a renaissance of the arts and sciences?

We British people for many generations have been fortunate in our Royal women. They have served us well and in turn we have given them a devotion that has kept alive the spirit of Chivalry.

Our Royal Family symbolize for us the perfection all would like to attain.

All round the Queen are men who have risen to the summit of their professions through hard work—but she towers over them simply from right of birth. And they accept this.

It is one of the strengths of the British Constitution that the Queen sits easily upon the top rung of the ladder others have to climb with such endeavor, so that however high a man may mount there is always someone above him—a man or woman who took that place, not after a lifetime of application, but by inheriting it as a natural birthright.

Onlookers from the outside, who have not thought deeply on the matter, sometimes suppose that Great Britain is a country rigidly bound by convention, that "class" barriers prevent a man from rising to high estate.

That is not so.

A man may rise in Britain as quickly as he can in any other country. But whereas in another land he may well start life in the traditional log cabin and end up as President, in England he will never start in a pre-fab and end up in Buckingham Palace.

There is no competitive scramble for the highest position of all. It cannot be won by merit or bought by favors; it is above and apart from all such considerations.

The Queen is not just one of us, serving for personal

success. She represents all of us. Her influence is not factional but is above factions, maintaining the balance among classes and interests. And maintaining it not by inactive example but by knowledge and experience.

Queen Elizabeth can rightly refer to Britain as "My Country," for indeed she is its head, apex to a pyramid of achievement, which depends as much on her crowning it as she depends on it to support her.

It is a curious thing about our Constitution that she is automatically head on earth of the Church, in which no woman can hold office, and patron of a dozen societies and professions about which her knowledge can be no more than any other layman's.

But all this gives a focus to public life. To have one head of all manner of professions gives them a unity and strength which a dozen competing leaders might disrupt.

The Throne is a central point toward which all thoughts turn, a concentration of power channeling it through one narrow opening where it can be harnessed to the best use.

But never before has this power been invested in such a human personality as Queen Elizabeth the Second. True, Queen Victoria came to the Throne quickly, as did Queen Elizabeth in the great and glorious days of the sixteenth century.

But the conventions have changed since then, and new developments have come to the institution of monarchy, enhancing rather than diminishing its influence.

The old Queen Elizabeth had more power of the "off with his head" kind. Queen Victoria may have, in her later years, exercised a firm but kindly rule over many sides of British life; but neither of them came to power with such love and admiration as Queen Elizabeth commands.

For she is a Queen of a more modern and lovable school than either of the others.

In her straightforward, heart-warming way she has gone out among people in a fashion unthinkable at any other time in the history of the British Monarchy. No other Heir to the Throne had that same contact with the ordinary man and woman as Queen Elizabeth so rightly demanded since she left the schoolroom and satisfied her longing to know how people lived outside the Palace walls.

With a home and children of her own, she has made it her business to know what other people's homes are like and how they live.

Those of you who read *Mother and Queen* will remember how I spoke of the way in which Queen Mary broke through much of the red tape which surrounded a woman of the Royal Family. Queen Elizabeth has followed in her footsteps and gone a good deal further.

At the age of sixteen she insisted on being allowed to join the A.T.S., and there obtained a valuable insight into the lives of other women, a knowledge she could never have picked up from a lifetime of tours and inspections.

From the very first she has been interested in the problems which confront people outside palace walls. Like her parents, she has a deep concern for the underprivileged.

She hates to think of people suffering, or being denied sustenance or comfort. Although as Queen she must remain above politics, it is certain that she will always keep an eye open for the rights of the individual.

Then, after those invaluable months in the Army, where for the first time the public saw or read of a Princess lying on her back in oil-stained overalls, tinkering with the engine of a lorry, she married Prince Philip.

As I have shown, that was a love match comparable with any in fiction. It is a beautiful and wonderful thing that Queen Elizabeth should have found in the man she loves a new and refreshing source of contact with the kind of people she will rule over.

The Duke of Edinburgh's life has not been led behind cloistered walls. He has lived always among men of action, whose thoughts and feelings he can translate to the Queen, giving her an insight she would never have been able to gather in any other way.

There is no doubt that the position of the Throne has undergone great development and expansion in the past fifty years. Britain's Royal Family have gone through some hard times in the history of the past few centuries. Never have they been so loved and so much part of their people's lives as they are today.

When they visited South Africa on that triumphal tour of 1947, such was their charm that even the Republican critics who most keenly attacked them, were silenced by it and completely won over.

Queen Elizabeth has that natural dignity so necessary to a position which makes her the center of all eyes wherever she goes, she has the charm and personality which make people warm to her as a person regardless of her rank, and she has a profound background knowledge about the meaning of her position in the world.

I often used to think, as I watched Princess Elizabeth leading a long line of dancers round the Palace ballrooms during those informal evening parties she so enjoyed, that this was an entirely new view of Royalty.

Not for her the distant dignity which makes the Throne a thing of awe, and sometimes terrifying. She prefers that human approach more in keeping with the times and her own modern temperament.

Queen Victoria may have loved to dance herself, and certainly did so with her beloved Prince Consort, but can you imagine her so throwing off the solemnity of her position as to lead a cheerful romp of that nature? I cannot. In every way Queen Elizabeth's nature proves her to be a Woman of Her Time.

It was she who insisted that her husband should be allowed to rejoin the Navy and continue the career he loved rather than stay at home and help her with her manifold duties.

And then, with a humanity which warmed many hearts, she flew out to him as soon as she could to catch for a little while the delight any wife takes in her husband's presence.

All this places her in an entirely personal position in British hearts. No one can feel about her that she is just a figurehead. She is too alive, too warm, too vital ever to be thought of in that way.

There are many State duties on the highest level which the Queen has to perform. All State documents must be signed by her. It is part of the law of the land that no Statute passed by Parliament is legal until signed by the Sovereign.

And though the Queen cannot refuse to sign, she will no doubt exercise the power of advice and suggestion so often used by her Royal ancestors.

Each sovereign in turn, from his permanent status and his long knowledge of affairs of State, commands a wide area of experience.

Crises have come and gone and our Kings and Queens throughout the years have known how to deal with them.

Now I think it is safe to quote a distinguished South African who said, after observing Princess Elizabeth throughout the Royal Family's tour of the dominion: "If there are still Queens when she comes to inherit the Throne, I think she will make the greatest one of all. . . ."

204 ·

Supplement

An Editor's Note About

THE QUEENS BEFORE ELIZABETH

I

MATILDA, the only legitimate daughter of Henry I and a granddaughter of William the Conqueror, was the first woman to hold the throne of England. While England's first sovereign queen never earned for herself an imposing niche in world history, her son, Henry II, for whom she fought relentlessly during her lifetime, became one of England's most notable rulers.

A miserable childhood passed in the shadow of a cruel father and an abused mother was Matilda's preparation for a life of violence and bloodshed. The only brightness in her early years was the love she had for her little brother William, the king-to-be. The two children had the fresh complexions, the fair hair, and the blue eyes of their northern forebears. They were devoted to each other. The fact that she was, according to the royal laws of inheritance, entirely subordinate to her brother never bothered Matilda; she expected nothing more, she wanted no more.

The royal children were trained by the same tutors. While William recited his Latin and stumbled through the intricacies of theology and philosophy, Matilda also absorbed much of the discipline by which rulers are formed. Of the two she was the apter pupil, more eager to learn, less distracted by the sports of hunting and tilting which beckoned to the boy through the schoolroom windows.

Then tragedy struck. Returning from a visit to France in a beautiful ship all painted white to match the innocence of its precious cargo, William was separated from his sister forever. The ship struck a rock and sank at once, carrying the little boy with it to the bottom of the stormy English Channel. For days no one in England dared to tell the King. Finally courtiers dressed a little page boy all in black, and sent him alone and weeping bitterly into Henry's presence. When the father at last realized the news, he fell from his raised chair to the floor in a swoon. And shortly he, too, was dead.

Before his death he seems to have finally recognized some of his paternal duties. He saw that Matilda got a husband, Geoffrey Plantagenet, Count of Anjou, one of the most powerful nobles of France. And he made his own barons swear allegiance to Matilda as his heir and their future queen.

The oath was kept by the barons only so long as their

sovereign lived. Matilda's marriage had united two great French provinces (she inherited the province of Normandy), but the barons hated the Count and had often been at war with him. When Henry's nephew Stephen appeared in England, claiming the throne as his, many of the barons who had sworn loyalty to Matilda went over to his side.

Civil war broke out. Matilda rallied the nobles who remained faithful to her, and planned a campaign. The birth of her little son encouraged her. She was crowned by the clergy in 1141 and accepted by the citizens of London, who welcomed her as the daughter of a queen they had loved.

She was aided by the faithlessness, the arrogance, the stupidity of Stephen himself. She was aware of the pitfalls into which bright promises can lure weak men. She knew Stephen, and she waited until the inevitable moment when he would go too far. Then she struck. While she led her army in England, her husband fought for her in her French kingdom of Normandy.

For fifteen years the conflict raged intermittently. The times were brutal. Prisoners would be blinded or mutilated if they were not lucky enough to be killed. The master of a castle would be starved in front of his family and retainers until they yielded the fortress out of compassion. Churches full of women and children would be locked, then set afire. Sometimes Stephen's side won, more often Matilda's.

At length the young Henry came of age and, in 1148,

Matilda could retire from the contest. Weary and sick of the reckless outrages of the war, she was glad to find peace at last in a nook of the French countryside near her ailing husband. Emerging only once, to demand on the death of Stephen's son that the English acknowledge her Henry as the next king, she was then content to forfeit her own rights and quickly disappear from public life.

II

Four hundred years were to flow beneath the bridge of history before another woman occupied the throne of England. A more unhappy woman, more thwarted, more vilified, has seldom been forced to endure the pain of high position.

Her father a supreme egoist, a man so raging with the zest of life that he brushed aside scruples like buzzing flies, an epicure in love, war, art and politics, Mary Tudor began her life under a double handicap: she was ugly and she was a girl. The flamboyant Henry VIII who begot her cared only for beauty and wanted only a son. And just as she reached the age when a happy family relationship is vital to any child, her father divorced her mother.

The marriage had been doomed from the first. Katherine, daughter of Columbus's Ferdinand and Isabella, aunt of the Pope, bred in the rigid code of Spanish court etiquette, was no mate for the bluff and burly English king. It had been a political marriage; love had played a minor role, if any. Katherine had seen her first husband sicken in his youth and die. And after Mary's birth in 1516 she had seen her babies—some boys among them—die too. Far away from her people, embittered by injustice, she retreated into the comfort and consolation of her religion, far from her carefree husband.

Then a blow that changed the world. Her divorce and the outlawing of her religion in this cold land of her exile. Katherine of Aragon clung to her daughter and drew the child with her into her resentful retirement.

From this distance the girl saw her father marry and dispose of wife after wife, saw her hopes for the throne, whereby she might restore justice and faith, vanish with the birth of her half-brother Edward, saw her religion debased and its adherents martyred. Small wonder that she grew into a tight-lipped, hard-featured woman obsessed with a burning zeal to rehabilitate her injured mother's dignity and creed.

Fate stepped into Mary's life with the unexpected death of the boy king Edward VI, her half-brother. He had left no heir. His dying plea, that his Protestant cousin Lady Jane Grey succeed him, was forgotten before he was buried; and that lovely, luckless girl was beheaded as a traitor.

The joy with which Mary, the oldest of her father's children, was welcomed to the throne did much to sweeten her nature. The people, bewildered by their enforced change of religion from Catholic to Protestant, longed for their old familiar ceremonies which Mary would restore. The people, her people, were with her. For the first time in her life she felt wanted and happy.

Joyously she announced her choice of a husband—her cousin Philip II of Spain, the champion of Catholicism on the continent against the threats of the Protestant Reformation. In spite of opposition from the English, even a mild rebellion, Mary still revelled in her happiness. Philip, whom she had never seen, came to England to claim his bride, and she met him brimming with love.

But her happiness was shortlived. Philip was a dour, silent Spaniard, cold and gloomy as the monastery palace he was building for himself outside Madrid. He had no love for Mary. He admitted openly that she revolted him. After vainly trying to keep up appearances, though he avoided even seeing Mary as much as he could, he sailed back to Spain and his own black introspection.

Disappointment followed on disappointment for the hapless, lonely queen. The strategically vital port of Calais on the French side of the Channel was suddenly besieged by a French army and irrevocably lost to England.

Furthermore, Mary was encountering opposition to her plans to restore Catholicism in England. The Protestant fires burned brighter the more she tried to quench them. In her now-frantic obsession to vindicate her mother and her faith she consigned nearly three hundred Protestant leaders to the flames. The popularity she had so recently enjoyed curdled in front of her.

Nor were her only tortures political or diplomatic ones. Her health, never too good—she was always of a sallow, dull complexion—began to fail, and she suffered physical agonies. Her desire to bear a child unfulfilled, she fell a prey to embarrassing psychic pregnancies. Placards appeared against her in the streets, threatening letters were thrown into her very room, almost daily plots against her life were discovered, she was cruelly ridiculed for her childlessness and for the husband who had deserted her, yet whom she loved even more than ever.

A woman of weaker principles, of softer faith, might have capitulated or compromised. Mary was too strong, too courageous in her faith that heretics were unworthy to live upon a good earth, ever to yield to so ephemeral a consolation as popularity. Her measures were the measures of her time, comparable to those of any other contemporary monarch, easily defensible. Whether we side with her or not, a detached objective judgment of her cannot fail to praise her singleness of purpose and steadfastness of spirit.

III

Mary died, raving, and exclaiming that if her body were to be opened, the word *Calais* would appear chiseled on her heart. At her death in 1558 her half-sister Elizabeth began the long reign which was to bring England an empire, make her mistress of the seas, and for the first time in her five-hundred-year-old history a world power.

The thin-faced, sharp-featured, red-haired Elizabeth was the daughter of Henry VIII by his second wife Anne Boleyn, a woman of vaguely royal blood, high spirit, education and, above all, charm. Anne suited her temperamental husband; in fact, of all his six wives, she was probably the only one he truly loved, and in their scant three years together only one thing blemished their carefree life—Anne's inability to produce the male heir Henry, now determined to found a dynasty, demanded. Her second child, a boy, died at birth.

Shortly thereafter charges of adultery were trumped up against her at the instigation of the impatient Henry. Witnesses were tortured into accusing her, and Anne, whose only true fault had been her ambition to be queen in spite of the risk involved, was sent to the Tower of London, where she was beheaded.

Elizabeth grew up among guardians appointed by her royal father, some of whom treated her with ribald disrespect; others, knowing that some day she would rule them, with deference and sincere interest in her development. Among the latter group was her tutor, the scholarly, humane Roger Ascham, whose little book, *The Schoolmaster*, is a classic of educational procedure. Another was her last stepmother, Queen Katherine Parr, who supplied for a few years the only motherly guidance Elizabeth was to know.

The Queens Before Elizabeth

She was a clever girl. She learned to speak Latin as fluently as she did her own tongue, not to mention Greek and French. She mastered the intricate steps of the dances of her time, as energetic and exhausting as a track meet in ours, and she performed with skill on the virginals. Like her father, she could compose poetry (though not so well as he) and sing it to her own accompaniment. Above all she learned the art of government, the cultivation of which in her time was as ardently pursued as the quest for charm in ours.

Government, to the sixteenth-century Renaissance Englishmen, meant far more than the negotiations of politics. It was the science of self-control, self-discipline, self-development. Based on the principle that he who can govern himself can rule over many, it was the foundation of the code of the gentleman, the nobleman, the Christian.

Elizabeth was trained, in short, to be a gentleman. And her time held its standards for gentlemen high. A gentleman was a complete man, a human being who had developed to the utmost all his talents as a tribute to Him who had bestowed them. A gentleman was to be a scholar and a man of action, a poet and a scientist, a soldier and a cavalier. It is surprising how many could fill the bill. Down through the ages have come the names of Sidney and Raleigh, Bacon and Essex and Drake, Ben Jonson and Thomas More—all of whom and more met well the exacting demands.

Perhaps it was because for the first time in history

· 215

any man could be a gentleman. The old feudal barriers of class had melted away, and in the new free society, as in the early days of our own nation, a man could rise from guttersnipe to governor if he chose. The legend of Dick Whittington, Elizabeth's contemporary, is based upon actual fact.

The tranquillity of Elizabeth's schoolroom, however, was frequently stirred by the turmoil that seethed around her. From one day to the next she did not know for certain who her father was, as Henry VIII, consulting the expediency of the moment, first denied then confirmed her legitimacy. It made her nervous. At times she was treated as a Princess of England, at others like a common criminal under heavy guard. She even knew the terror of the Tower, aware that any dawn might bring her to the headsman's block. She was trusted and suspected, consulted and spied upon. Conditions which might easily have brought a mental collapse to a weaker soul Elizabeth turned to her own ends and emerged from her trials, like Minerva from the head of Jove, full-grown, full-armed, full of knowledge of the tricks of this world and fully aware of the temper of her people.

The time of troubles under Edward VI and Mary had left England tired and poor, the people bewildered and diffident. Elizabeth saw as her first task the restoration of peace, plenty, and confidence. Restraining the love of lavishness she had inherited from her father, she declared a period of rest, rehabilitation, and economy. For thirty years England was to know no major war, no unsettling embroilments. Knowing well the heart-quickening thrill of a parade, Elizabeth spent her time touring her country, showing herself in splendor in the remotest hamlets, winning the love of her people, the vast majority of whom had never seen their sovereign, had at best merely heard her name.

For Elizabeth had the personal charm that belongs only to people of great character. How can this charm be defined? One can only say, with J. M. Barrie, it's that something which if you have it, it doesn't matter what you haven't; and if you haven't it, it doesn't matter what you have. Because of her charm, people forgot that she was iron-willed, uncompromising, often cruel, a tyrant. For tyrants without charm might as well put up their shutters. One shudders to think what might have happened if Hitler had had the personal charm of Elizabeth.

Yet Elizabeth has many deeds to account for before some judgment bar. She sent her cousin Mary Queen of Scots to the block, and her lover and warrior Essex. She broke faith and she nurtured grievances. She stole, she swore, and she lied. She managed, however, to convince the world that she did all these things out of love for her people and on behalf of England.

The praise that was lavished upon her by the writers she encouraged, whose works may outlive her memory —Shakespeare, Spenser, Marlowe, Bacon, Jonson, Sidney, Beaumont, Nash, Greene, and countless others— makes a cynic wonder whether it was the price they paid for their success, if not their lives. Hardly. These men were popular successes, too, and the people of no age will stand for tributes to a character they dislike. Elizabeth had given them a nation in which they could take pride, had spread the glory of England around the globe, had made the words "I am an Englishman" a passport in every land.

Under her shrewd guidance, not the least part of which was her uncanny ability to choose good men to serve her and bring out the best in them, England had beaten Spain, her chief rival and the Russia of her times. For the last fifteen years of her reign had not been years of peace. On the seas, on the continent of Europe, in the Western Hemisphere, English blood had been spilled and many of England's—Elizabeth's—sons had laid their good lives down.

It saddened their mother-image, the queen, old queen now. Her red hair had dropped out, and she wore a wig. Her teeth had rotted in her head. Lines and wrinkles had made her long, pointed face witchlike. Frightened to behold herself, she decreed that there should be no mirrors in her palaces. She had craved human love, but her yearnings had fought with duty and lost, leaving her heart broken. And she feared for the country to which she had devoted her life, feared for its welfare in the hands of her silly Scottish cousin who must succeed her since she had not been able to yield to even the domination of marriage and hence was childless.

She had come to the throne, like the present Queen,

when she was twenty-five, and she had reigned for
forty-five years. She was tired. One winter's day in 1603
a stroke deprived her of her speech and stretched her
on the floor where, unable to move or be moved, she
lingered a few days. Anger flashed from her eyes that
she should be brought low by any power, even Nature's. Her last gesture was to raise her hands feebly
above her head to signify a crown.

IV

Eighty years later, in the palace of Richmond, two
young girls waited for the weekly visit of their handsome young father, the Duke of York, brother of the
King.

Mary Stuart, the older of the two, was busy at her
painting, guided by her dwarf teachers. Nearby her
sister Anne played cards for high stakes with her beloved playmate, Sarah Jennings. From time to time
the two princesses would leave their pastimes, cross the
room to a table laden with cakes and candied fruits
which they could not leave alone. Mary was the taller
of the two, nearly six feet in her low slippers, a handsome girl with a magnificent figure and eyes as bright
as the jewels on her full breasts. Anne had already let
her passion for food swell her shorter stature beyond
the limits of neatness.

Presently the Duke, accompanied by the girls' mater-
nal grandfather, the Earl of Clarendon, elder statesman
of his time, entered the room. Mary ran to her father

and kissed him. It was plain to see that she was his favorite. Anne received a kiss from her grandfather, who cherished her because in face, nature, and name, she was the image of his dead daughter, the girl's mother.

Politely Mary inquired in fluent French after the health of her new Italian stepmother, who had stayed behind because she was expecting a baby. She talked of the history she had been studying, played on the harpsichord the new sonata Henry Purcell had written for her, demonstrated the graceful steps she had just learned from her French dancing master.

Anne sullenly sat by, nibbling at yet another cake. A true child of the stolid Puritan Clarendons, she had neither her sister's grace nor her brains. And she resented the pretty young Queen, both for her Roman Catholic religion and for her lack of consideration in conceiving a child who would stand between the sisters and the throne, for her Uncle Charles had no legitimate heir of his own.

Mary finished her entertainment and seated herself at her father's knee. A hush fell on the room as he stroked her light brown hair. Feeling that intimate and important matters were at hand, the playmates and the dwarfs stole quietly away. Then James, the Duke, spoke to his daughter.

There was war in Europe, he told her, and English trade was suffering. The one man who could make peace and restore the economic life of their country was her cousin, the Prince of Holland, William of Orange. If Mary would marry him, he would act to save her people's revenues. Would she?

Mary burst into tears. She was only fifteen, too young to marry anyone, let alone this old man of thirty who she had heard was morose and bad-tempered. And she would have to leave her beloved England, her dear sister, her even dearer father, to dwell among strangers.

Patiently James explained to her that such was the duty of a royal girl. Her grandfather added that it was the will of her sovereign uncle the King. There was nothing for her to do but give in. Anne tried to comfort her.

The plans for the marriage went ahead, and each new plan was a fresh disappointment for Mary. There was not even to be a state wedding. Instead, a few close relatives gathered in a room of St. James's palace at night. Anne was grievously sick of the smallpox, and the Queen was already in labor. The King was present, but he spoiled everything when, hurrying the business along, he said: "Come, Bishop, make all the haste you can, lest my sister, the Duchess of York, should bring us a boy to disappoint the marriage." A day later little James Stuart was born, and in a fortnight Mary sailed off to The Hague with her husband.

On the voyage William humiliated her by taking a mistress from among Mary's ladies-in-waiting. When they arrived, he refused her the English religious services she had requested (eventually she turned her dining room into a chapel and ate in the pantry). She was kept virtually a prisoner in a gloomy palace. William even denied her the day, sacred to all Stuarts, of fasting and mourning in commemoration of the martyrdom of Charles I; instead, he forced her to entertain at a state banquet for some petty diplomat. She yearned for her father, and the news that her husband had sent a fleet against him (albeit at the request of the English, who feared a Catholic heir to the throne) sent her to bed, sick with grief.

Soon, however, she was to return to her native land as queen, joint ruler with her husband. The unlucky James had fled from William's fleet, escaping to France in an open boat which received him from some back stairs of his palace on the Thames. Joyfully she entered the palace and ransacked it to get rid of her stepmother's property. From his exile her father wrote, cursing her.

Her six years' reign was unhappy. Even her coronation was badly arranged. Neither Mary nor William had been provided with so much as a penny to put in the offering; an engraver, loyal to James, had struck commemorative medals that were a savage caricature of the new sovereigns. Soon she quarreled bitterly with Anne over money matters, and refused to see her sister again. She took up gambling to hide her sense of failure. She was almost burned up in a palace fire. Plots on her life constantly threatened her. The people jeered at her and forced her to repeal the Sunday blue laws she had made, since they knew she was incapable of keeping them herself.

Yet she was by no means incompetent. In William's absences fighting against his father-in-law—and he was in England barely four months a year—she had full power, which she exercised with decision and vigor. She negotiated the political union of Scotland with England. She rallied and reorganized the English fleet, after its shattering defeat at Beachy Head, and sent it on to a glorious victory over the French at La Hogue. She founded the Naval Hospital at Greenwich. She recaptured the respect of her people with her beauty and, like Elizabeth, her awareness of the morale-building effect of a good show.

Falling ill of a disease which could not at once be diagnosed, she dosed herself with cordials stronger than brandy. The sickness turned out to be measles, but she was past thirty, and she had, suspecting the worst, sat up all one night to destroy incriminating papers. This and her own doctoring killed her, eight years before her husband, in the year 1694.

Mary had died childless, and on the death of William in 1702 the throne passed to Anne, who for fifteen years had lived in the blighting shadow of her sister and brother-in-law.

Her subordination had not improved her abilities,, her health, or her temper. Always inclined to be frivolous, she had never learned even to write good English. Her passion for food had made her enormously fat, gouty, and dropsical, so that she could not even stand at her coronation; in fact most of her mature life she was carried about in an armchair. She had become the puppet of her strong-willed, acidulous playmate Sarah Jennings—they played a continuous game in which they called each other Mrs. Freeman and Mrs. Morley—and had learned from her to be gossipy, spiteful, and vulgar. She had been deeply humiliated when her cousin (later George I) came to propose to her and ran home shocked. She forsook her father's cause and joined the party that forced him off the throne. On the night of his flight she went to a scandalous play, and when she heard the news of his deposition merely called for cards and fell to gambling.

Her marriage, also negotiated by Charles II, to Prince George of Denmark, was happier than Mary's, but it brought her grief. Seven of her eight children died at birth, or in infancy. One reached the age of eleven—a charming and clever boy—before he was carried off by an ill-doctored cold. Her husband died seven years later.

These blows sobered her. She regarded the death of her son as a judgment upon her for her ill treatment of her own father, and made amends to him. She patched up her quarrel with King William. She tried to give up gambling. In her sweet, thrilling voice she proclaimed to her people at her accession: "As I know my heart to be entirely English, I can very sincerely assure you there is not anything you can desire of me which I shall not be ready to do for the prosperity of England."

Thus she embarked upon a thirteen years' reign which rivalled Elizabeth I's in glory. In cold historical fact, however, little credit for its brilliance can be directly attributed to Anne. Much of the sovereign's power and influence had been constitutionally diverted to the ministers of state. These able men had sometimes to restrain Anne from measures that would have made her reign a failure, such as her wish to dismiss the great general Marlborough, husband of Sarah Jennings, with whom Anne had violently quarreled.

The campaigns of this ancestor of Winston Churchill won glory for England in Europe and in North America. At home, the freedoms of the new constitution and the rivalries of the two-party system stimulated the literary masterpieces of Alexander Pope and Jonathan Swift, of Addison and Steele, of Defoe and Congreve. The work of Sir Isaac Newton was revising old concepts of the universe; the architecture of Sir Christopher Wren was setting the style for hundreds of years.

Anne seems to have been unaffected by this flowering of talent. Harassed by her ill health, hounded by remorse, lonely and friendless, she shut off the last years of her life from the busy world around her to grieve for the fate of her exiled family. Her last words were a prayer for the half-brother she had once resented and abused.

V

In the gray dawn of a June morning in 1837 the Archbishop of Canterbury and the Lord Chancellor of England knelt before a short, slim eighteen-year-old girl in a dressing gown and announced to her that she was Queen of England. Calmly and fearlessly she replied: "I will be good."

So began the sixty-three-year reign—longest of British sovereigns—of Queen Victoria, great-great-grandmother of Queen Elizabeth the Second.

The news came not unexpectedly to the round-faced, doll-pretty girl. Nor did it find her unprepared. As they had watched the people who stood between Victoria and the throne die heirless one by one, her mother and her governess Lehzen had intensified their already rigorous discipline. She had been trained, with the German thoroughness common to both women, in simple ideals, in self-control, in devotion to duty above all. And as Victoria herself had gradually recognized her destiny, she had acquired a sense of responsibility unusual in a girl of her age and a determination to carry well the burden of the crown.

In spite of the domination of her tutors Victoria had a mind and a will of her own. Her first command as queen was that she have a room separate from her mother's. It was an order that symbolized not only her independence, but also her perception that she had until then been guided too much by books, too little by experience. Her mother and the Baroness Lehzen were simple and provincial women from a petty German state, knowing little of the problems that would confront the ruler of a world power of the first magnitude. Far more clearly than they Victoria had glimpsed the enormity of her task and the necessity of making her own decisions.

Immediately, however, she encountered an immovable obstacle. Her training seemed to have omitted the fact that rulers were no longer arrogant Tudor despots whose frown could doom an unlucky man to the headsman's block. For two hundred years gradual changes in the English Constitution had eventually succeeded in rendering the sovereign's personal power nonexistent. The imperious, impetuous girl had to curb her will in the face of laws which, as the constitutional changes continued, more and more restrained her own wishes. She had to learn to yield to the persuasion of her great statesmen.

Patiently she submitted to the gentle, sophisticated advice of her first Prime Minister, Lord Melbourne, as he explained that laws for her kingdom must be made according to expediency, not by the ideal theories she had been accustomed to. She submitted, but she never yielded, no more than she did to any other human being, whether it was her mother, the great statesmen who managed her government—Melbourne, Disraeli,

Palmerston, Gladstone, Salisbury—or her own beloved husband Albert. The conflict harassed her throughout her lifetime.

It might have been simpler for her to give up, but the easy way out of a dilemma was not Victoria's way or the way of life she wished to impart to her people. Thwarted in governing according to idealistic principles, she found a new definition for royal duty. She would be an example for her people to follow. She would set a standard for the fundamentals which are above law and on which all civilized societies are built —love, family, home, propriety.

In the fifty years before Victoria's accession England had fallen on evil times. Long wars had weakened morale, and the false prosperity they had brought had corrupted principles. The standards once set by the aristocracy had declined with the aristocrats themselves —class suicide, perhaps, or victims of the selfish, aggressive factory owners and merchants who had risen to power and prominence on the inrushing tide of new industry. Victoria's uncle, George IV, both as regent for his insane father and as king, was dissolute, depraved, degenerate. Society had followed him in making vice fashionable and virtue intolerable. Her other uncle, William IV, was too old and tired to cope with the unbridled demands of the new classes and let them have their way.

All this Victoria set about to amend. She married for love a distant cousin, Prince Albert of Saxe-Coburg, and she continued to adore him until she died long after him. Together they established a home life with their eight children which was a pattern of such domestic bliss that it was everywhere envied and emulated.

Studiously Albert revised their household economy and re-established it on a frugal and sensible basis. He encouraged Victoria to study governmental issues so that her understanding of them, through the abstracts he painstakingly prepared for her, confounded the politicians who attempted to sway her judgment. He awoke in her a sensitivity to beauty so that together they might encourage a flourishing of the arts which spread abroad the prestige of a country more indelibly than its battles. Together they rode or drove through the parks of London; together they explored the beauties of the Scottish highlands they loved, stopping often to paint a particularly pretty view. They found their amusements at home, reading to each other and their children, fondling their pets, playing the piano, and singing. Victoria was fond of dancing, and Albert loved hunting. Innocent pleasures they found and proved to be the most rewarding. The first Elizabeth had displayed herself to her people as a glittering monarch surpassing their wildest dreams of splendor. Victoria and Albert showed themselves as a devoted couple, secure in simple ways that even the humblest of their subjects could achieve. In almost every home hung reproductions of paintings that represented the Queen and her family in their unpretentious happiness.

Their encouragement sustained the genius of great writers: Dickens, Thackeray, Meredith, Hardy, and Kipling as story tellers. Browning, Tennyson, Matthew Arnold, Swinburne, and Hopkins as poets. Philosophy and history throve in the hands of Carlyle and Macaulay, Ruskin and Spencer. The drama revived with the plays of Pinero, Jones, Wilde, and Shaw. In painting there were the names of Turner, Rossetti, Millais, Burne-Jones, Hunt, Alma-Tadema, Watts, Brown, and Landseer. The music of Elgar, Sullivan and Mendelssohn still graces our most sacred rituals. In science Darwin and Huxley and Lyall dispelled ancient superstitions about man's origin and the earth's. And all these products were infused with the principle of the Royal Couple that improvement of the mind and the character is the justification of art.

Many readers of these pages saw the last flickers of this great age which took its name from a little woman who, as the years passed, became fat, red-faced, and jowly; whom few people saw but whose power was felt by millions. For although actually powerless herself, she exerted a power greater than that of any other English queen. Elizabeth may have inspired her subjects to more brilliant achievements, but they could never become one with her as they could with Victoria. In Victoria's submission to law she became an influence that penetrated into the remotest corners of the vast empire that was hers. She ruled more truly and more permanently than any other monarch.

Other readers, brought up according to the principles of this great Victorian age, may have come to resent it or to laugh at it. In its own lack of humor, it had its humorous side. Victoria's own "We are not amused," and her preoccupation with trifles (such as sailors' mustaches) when the fate of a nation hung in the balance, can scarcely be taken without a smile today. Her lofty standards produced a certain hypocrisy in those who claimed to be scrupulously following them. Her tendency to avoid realities by hiding them under non-functional ornament sometimes produced disastrous results. The paintings, the poems, and the music she loved we accuse of flagrant sentimentality or of unjustified optimism. Yet today Victorian styles are again in fashion, reminding us of years that were solid and strong, representing our pathetic craving for the peace and security Victoria gave her people.

She gave them also a sense of importance, great national pride, invincible authority. She was at the head of an empire which her statesmen had built for her and on which the sun never set. Her battle lines were flung into Africa, Asia, and the seas beyond. When Disraeli crowned her Empress of India, she surveyed a dominion larger than Alexander's, Caesar's, Charlemagne's, or Napoleon's, larger than any ever known before or since.

But the power and the glory meant little to her, for Albert was dead and she was inconsolable. For twenty years she withdrew to the castle in Scotland where they had spent such happy hours together and where every clump of heather held a teardrop memory of her beloved husband. She erected a huge and unique memorial to him near the palace of her girlhood and facing the great hall and museum to which she gave his name. She preserved everything that had in any sense been connected with him, and she gave instructions that nothing, not even a chair, was to be moved from the spot to which Albert had assigned it. In the lonely sorrow of her widowhood she wrote his Life, and worked on the memoirs of her own that had been so formed by him.

Their line had gone out to all the earth. Their children were kings and queens, and begot kings and queens. Her great jubilee celebrations of 1887 and 1897 brought tributes pouring in from every land. Still she had to accept them alone, without Albert. The joyful gratitude of her people on these occasions may have softened her resentment of the bombs that had been thrown at her in her youth and the insults that had been offered her during her long retirement; but it could never wipe away the fact that they had disliked Albert because he was a German. She longed only to join him in some world where such disapproval could not exist.

Four years after her Diamond Jubilee her people again lined the streets to watch her pass by, this time in a tiny casket with six kings riding behind her. Few of them had ever known another sovereign. There was passing out of their lives a part of themselves, a part of England, a part of the world.

THE SOVEREIGNS OF ENGLAND

Sovereign	Relationship to Predecessor	Dates of Rule	Consort
HOUSE OF NORMANDY			
William I (the Conqueror)		1066–1087	Matilda of Flanders
William II (Rufus)	son	1087–1100	none
Henry I	brother	1100–1135	Matilda of Scotland, Adelicia of Louvain
Matilda	daughter	1135–1152	Geoffrey, Count of Anjou
HOUSE OF BLOIS			
Stephen	cousin	1135–1154	Matilda of Boulogne
HOUSE OF PLANTAGENET			
Henry II	nephew	1154–1189	Eleanor of Aquitaine
Richard I (the Lion-Heart)	son	1189–1199	Berengaria of Navarre
John	brother	1199–1216	Isabella of Angoulême
Henry III	son	1216–1272	Eleanor of Provence
Edward I	son	1272–1307	Eleanor of Castile, Marguerite of France
Edward II	son	1307–1327	Isabella of France
Edward III	son	1327–1377	Philippa of Hainault
Richard II	grandson	1377–1399	Anne of Bohemia, Isabella of Valois
HOUSE OF LANCASTER			
Henry IV	cousin	1399–1413	Joanna of Navarre
Henry V	son	1413–1422	Katherine of Valois
Henry VI	son	1422–1461	Margaret of Anjou
HOUSE OF YORK			
Edward IV	cousin	1461–1483	Elizabeth Woodville
Edward V	son	1483–1483	none
Richard III	uncle	1483–1485	Anne of Warwick
HOUSE OF TUDOR			
Henry VII	cousin	1485–1509	Elizabeth of York
Henry VIII	son	1509–1547	Katherine of Aragon, Anne Boleyn, Jane Seymour, Anne of Cleves, Katherine Howard, Katherine Parr

THE SOVEREIGNS OF ENGLAND

Sovereign	Relationship to Predecessor	Dates of Rule	Consort
Edward VI	son (by Jane Seymour)	1547–1553	none
Mary I	half-sister (by Katherine of Aragon)	1553–1558	Philip II of Spain
Elizabeth I	half-sister (by Anne Boleyn)	1558–1603	none
HOUSE OF STUART			
James I	cousin	1603–1625	Anne of Denmark
Charles I	son	1625–1649	Henrietta Maria of France
(The Commonwealth)			
Charles II	son	1660–1685	Catherine of Braganza
James II	brother	1685–1688	Anne Hyde / Mary Beatrice of Modena
William III } Mary I	nephew cousin (daughter of James II by Anne Hyde)	1688–1702 1688–1694	joint sovereigns
Anne	sister (daughter of James II by Anne Hyde)	1702–1714	Prince George of Denmark
HOUSE OF HANOVER			
George I	cousin	1714–1727	Sophia Dorothea of Zell
George II	son	1727–1760	Caroline of Anspach
George III	son	1760–1820	Charlotte of Mecklenburg
George IV	son	1820–1830	Caroline of Brunswick
William IV	brother	1830–1837	Adelaide of Saxe-Meinigen
Victoria	niece	1837–1901	Albert of Saxe-Coburg
HOUSE OF SAXE-COBURG			
Edward VII	son	1901–1910	Alexandra of Denmark
HOUSE OF WINDSOR			
George V	son	1910–1936	Mary of Teck
Edward VIII	son	1936–1936	no queen (later, as Duke of Windsor, married Wallis Simpson)
George VI	brother	1936–1952	Elizabeth Bowes-Lyon
Elizabeth II	daughter	1952–	Prince Philip of Greece

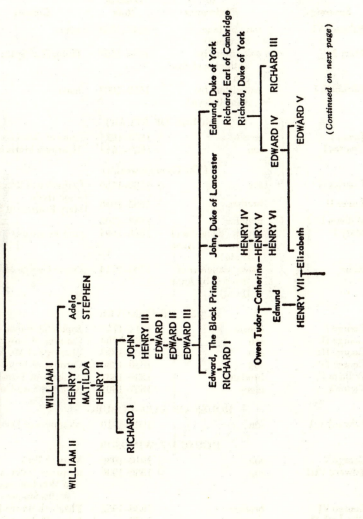

GENEALOGICAL TABLE OF ENGLISH SOVEREIGNS

WILLIAM I
WILLIAM II
Adela
STEPHEN
HENRY I
MATILDA
HENRY II
RICHARD I
JOHN
HENRY III
EDWARD I
EDWARD II
EDWARD III
Edward, The Black Prince
RICHARD I
John, Duke of Lancaster
HENRY IV
HENRY V
HENRY VI
Edmund, Duke of York
Richard, Earl of Cambridge
Richard, Duke of York
EDWARD IV
RICHARD III
EDWARD V
Owen Tudor—Catherine
Edmund
HENRY VII—Elizabeth

(Continued on next page)

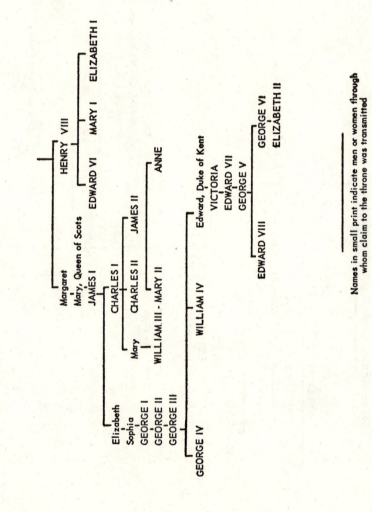

Names in small print indicate men or women through whom claim to the throne was transmitted